The
Cleveland
Village Book

THE VILLAGES OF BRITAIN SERIES

Other counties in this series include

Most are published in conjunction with
County Federations of Women's Institutes

The Cleveland Village Book

Compiled by the Cleveland
Federation of Women's Institutes from notes
and illustrations sent by Institutes in the County

Published jointly by
Countryside Books, Newbury
and the C.F.W.I., Middlesbrough

Countryside Books
3 Catherine Road
Newbury, Berkshire

ISBN 1 85306 139 5

Cover photograph of Egglescliffe parish church
taken by D. Thurman

Produced through MRM Associates Ltd., Reading
Typeset by Acorn Bookwork, Salisbury, Wilts
Printed in England by J.W. Arrowsmith Ltd., Bristol

Foreword

Cleveland, a county formed as a result of Local Government boundary changes, was at first called Teesside. Harald Hardrada, famous in Scandinavian Saga, is reputed to have said he landed in Yorkshire 'at that part that is called Cleveland'. It is generally understood that Cleveland means the Land of Cliffs. The county sits under the dramatic backdrop of the Cleveland Hills, its back washed by the North Sea, with the plains of South Durham on the northern side.

Cleveland could almost be called Changeland. They fought the Norman invaders until William laid waste to the North. They were sheep men and wool merchants, until they changed to agriculture. They farmed fish in man-made ponds. Then they found riches underground – potash at Boulby, followed by iron ore in the hills. This was married to coal from Durham and from this came the birth of Middlesbrough and of course the railways. Shipbuilding and heavy industry declined as the iron ore ran out. The next great giant on Cleveland was the giant chemical complex, providing a spectacular display of night-time lights and flares.

Despite all the industry Cleveland is a beautiful county, its miles of beaches and picture postcard villages unchanged in centuries, its castles, parks, museums and many international events renowned throughout the world. I hope that readers of this book will take the time and visit this diverse and beautiful county, that most visitors find is not quite what they expect. A big thank you to all the Members of Cleveland Federation of Women's Institutes and non-members who have contributed to this book.

Rosemary Billington
County Chairman

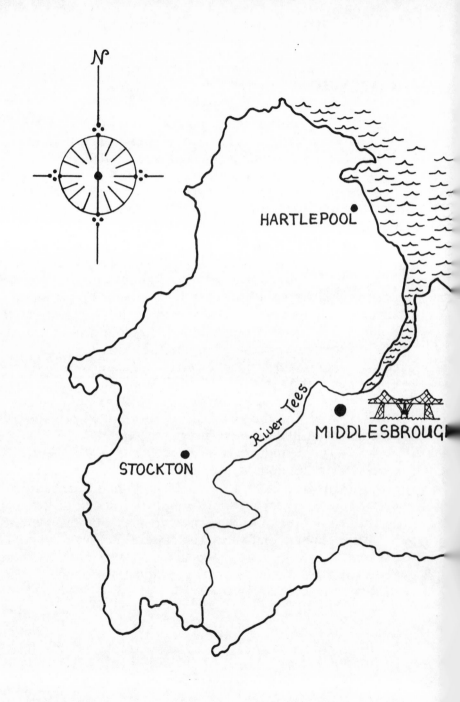

NORTH
SEA

REDCAR

SALTBURN

GUISBOROUGH

County of
CLEVELAND

Acknowledgements

The Federation of Cleveland Women's Institutes would like to thank all Institutes whose members have worked so hard to provide material for this book.

Also, thank you to the following:

Cleveland County Archaeology Department
Darchem Engineering, Stillington
I.C.I. Wilton
Local History Librarians
Cleveland Libraries
Middlesbrough Football Club

Finally, a special thank you to Doris Perley, the co-ordinator for this project.

Old cottages at Linthorpe

Acklam 🦢

Acklam is three miles south-west of Middlesbrough and is mentioned in the Domesday Book of 1086, when it was referred to as being almost all waste and taxable for 40 shillings. The land had not then recovered from the ravages of war 20 years previously. A church and a priest at Acklam is also mentioned in the Domesday Book.

Acklam was a rural community until the 20th century. In 1801 the population was 98, half of whom were engaged in agriculture. It is interesting to note that at this time the population of Middlesbrough was only 25. In 1931 the population had increased to 3,033, and in 1951 to 7,334 and in 1958 to over 10,000. The present population is 18,000.

Acklam manor was in the possession of Alvered in 1120 and it is through him that the estates can be traced to the Boyntons, who owned the manor until 1612 when it was leased to William Hustler and later, in 1637, sold to him. In 1929 Acklam Hall was sold by its owner Mr Mostyn Hustler to Middlesbrough Corporation for £11,500. In 1935 it was opened as a grammar school for boys and in 1967 Kirby Grammar School for girls combined with Acklam. When grammar schools were abolished the school divided into a comprehensive school and a sixth form college, with both schools sharing the main school complex. The school was renamed King's Manor when it opened in 1974.

Acklam Hall is the oldest domestic building in Middlesbrough. It was built about 1680 with an avenue of lime trees in front. A map of 1730 shows the avenue leading to Low Lane (A1044). The avenue was probably never used as an entrance drive, visitors would have approached by way of Acklam Road (A1032) and Hall Drive as this was a public thoroughfare from Stockton to Marske. Though a large number of the lime trees were blown down in a storm on the night of 7th January 1829, these were replaced and some still stand. The avenue is now about half a mile long with South Lodge at its end. This was built in 1912.

The grounds of the Hall were altered several times over the years with changes in fashion. At the end of the 17th century formal flower beds in geometrical shapes with narrow gravel paths and low box hedges were popular and this is shown in an engraving of Acklam Hall done in 1709. A century later the garden had changed and was landscaped with lawns, shrubs and trees. The water gardens of the previous century were made into a lake as the ground was low-lying and needed good drainage. The grounds were again changed in 1912 when Mr W. Goldring of Kew persuaded the owner to have the main drive rebuilt in a straight line from the avenue to the forecourt. The forecourt entrance had two large bronze lamps which have been removed to a place of safety.

The Hall still retains its magnificent staircase made from pine with carved twisted balusters and large square newel posts. The saloon which is now the school library has a beautiful plaster ceiling with wreaths, flying doves and griffons on it. The Royal Coat of Arms is also shown, probably because Charles II visited Acklam Hall on a private visit in 1684. A portrait of Charles II was displayed in the Hall and this is still owned by the Hustler family. A portrait of Nell Gwynne is also held by Mr Hustler who says that traditionally the two portraits must face each other or one of them falls down.

The Hall is reputed to have a ghost called the Grey Lady, but her identity has never been discovered.

St Mary's church is situated at the rear of the Hall. It is not known how many churches have stood on the site, but the present one was built in the early 1870s at the same time as a school was built at 281 Acklam Road. A supermarket stands on the site now. The church originally held only 135 people but as new houses were built in the area the church was extended in 1957 to hold 400 people. There are five memorial tablets of the Hustler family in the church, the latest being to William Thomas Hustler who died on 31st March 1909.

The oldest existing house in Middlesbrough still stands in Church Lane. It was built around 1730. There still exists a Devil's Bridge in the east of Acklam which carried a nearby track, probably from the Tees to Guisborough.

Aislaby 🌿

Aislaby got its name from a very old family called Aslackby, in the 13th century. Over the centuries there have been several different spellings of its name.

William D. Aslackby built and dedicated a chapel to St Thomas the Martyr in 1313. Remains of this chapel are still to be found at Aislaby Manor Farm.

The road which runs through the village was once the main road from Darlington to Yarm and the stage coaches would stop at the Black Bull (now no longer standing) for refreshments and also have their horses shod at the smithy – the dwelling is now called 'The Bungalow'. Drovers also used this road on their way to market. The local field labourers used to graze their sheep and goats on the green as it was common land.

As a lot of trading was done via the river, there used to be a landing stage at the bottom of the present green. At least two of the present dwellings are built with Dutch bricks, which were used as ballast on the ships. Most of today's residents are in business but there are still a few farms.

There is a story, handed down through the generations, that Oliver Cromwell once stopped at Aislaby. There were also several witches in the area and one called Sally Dodds put a curse on her uncle, who is reputed never to have got out of his bed again. The cottage where she lived is no longer there, another building having been erected on the site. There have also been recent sightings of a ghostly old man in gaiters and soft hat walking up the bank at the west end of the village with his collie dog.

Parish council meetings are held twice a year and the Minute Book used is the same one which was used when this council started at the end of the 19th century.

Aislaby is mentioned by Mother Shipton in her prophesies. She stated:

'When Yarm sinks and Egglescliffe swims
Aislaby will be the market town'.

A girl who lived at Aislaby East Farm in 1812 eloped to Gretna Green to be married. Her father, however, insisted on a proper marriage in the church. The bridegroom then boasted that he had been married twice before and had twelve children by his first wife. What a sad ending to her romantic escapade!

Billingham ✤

A visitor to Billingham today could be excused for thinking that this was a relatively new town, which had developed during the 20th century around a modern chemical industry. Although to some extent this is the case, exploration very soon reveals that there has been a settlement at Billingham for over a thousand years. Indeed, Billingham is among the oldest settlements on Teesside.

Evidence exists to prove that the Saxons were the first people to settle at Billingham in the late 8th or early 9th centuries. They found many acres of fertile low-lying land which abounded in plant and animal life, with fine views of the Yorkshire Hills across the river. They chose a small area of land to the south-west corner of the present large industrial town, where the village green and St Cuthbert's church stand today, because it was well drained and elevated away from the marshy area around the stream, which is now, and most certainly would be then, prone to flooding. In the year of AD 960, the church of St Cuthbert was built and the manor of Billingham became a possession of, and gave support to, the religious establishment of Durham.

From that time, for about a thousand years, the tiny village continued as an agricultural settlement with only a few hundred inhabitants. Life would continue along much the same lines throughout this time, unchanged except when some unexpected or tragic occurrence ruffled their lives – such as the Black Death, which came to Billingham in 1349, killing more than half of the population. The Dissolution of the Monasteries certainly had some effect on life in Billingham when Henry VIII had the Billingham manor confiscated and later, during the 1569 Northern Rebellion in support of Mary, Queen of Scots, several Billingham men were publicly executed because they remained faithful to their Roman Catholic beliefs.

By the end of the 19th century, there had been little development beyond the original medieval village, and those people who lived in Billingham in the early 20th century could hardly have imagined the tremendous changes that were soon to take place.

There are people alive today who well remember Billingham village as it was at that time. This was a close-knit community with a strong feeling of 'family' making for great loyalty. The church of St Cuthbert was, of course, the focal point of village life, with most of the modest dwellings clustered around the village green.

However, to the east of the green were some rather nice houses – the most dominant being the 18th century manor house, which was, at that time, occupied by Mr John Heslop, who owned a small brewery nearby. The village had its blacksmith's shop and a nearby mill, and a pinfold (a stray cattle pound) had existed on the south side of the green until the land was used for an extension to the village Church school in 1898. The Church of England school will be remembered with affection by many ex-pupils, as it was in use until the middle of the 20th century.

Standing at the lychgate of St Cuthbert's one would be confronted by two landmarks on the green: 'The Cross' and 'Robson's Folly'. The handsome cross was the idea of Rev Phillip Rudd, vicar of St Cuthbert's for most of the second half of the 19th century. The Prince of Wales, later to become Edward VII, was a fairly frequent visitor to Lord Londonderry's home at Wynyard and the story goes that the Prince had agreed to unveil The Cross en route to Wynyard Hall. A large crowd gathered, dressed in 'Sunday best' and waving Union Jacks, all ready to cheer the Royal prince. However to their dismay his carriage sped swiftly through the village without stopping at all. 'The Cross' has remained devoid of engraving to this day.

The story of 'Robson's Folly', often called Tower House or The Pinnacle, is rather amusing. 'The Folly' belonged to an unforgettable character of the village, George Robson, or as he was more commonly known, 'Taty' Robson because of his great knowledge and expertise on the growing of pota-toes. He had wanted to build along the west side of the green but was not allowed to do so by the local authorities. He is reputed to have said, 'If they won't let me build along then I'll build up', and so he did. The result was a white brick building 60 ft high, but with a base area of a small room.

A famous Billingham farming family were the Dixons of

Glebe Farm. They were expert and world-renowned plough-men, who won competitions throughout the British Isles and abroad. Tom Dixon won 262 ploughing championships and his son, Leslie followed in his footsteps, travelling to places as distant as Canada to compete.

These people of Billingham village were hard-working and on the whole rather poor, but they knew how to enjoy themselves when the opportunity arose. Holy Days and festivals were celebrated on the green. There was no dearth of alehouses, there being five or six around the green alone. The flooded area to the west of Billingham, known as Billingham Bottoms, froze over regularly in the winter, making it perfect for ice skating. People came from as far away as Middlesbrough and Hartlepool such was its popularity. The millers of Norton and Billingham hired out the skates and the hot potato and roast chestnut vendors set up their stalls.

Fancy dress parades and singing contests were popular, as well as cricket matches, football matches and races which were held on the green, with the whole village turning out to support these events.

Regrettably this pleasant rural way of life was destined to come to an end. The tremendous changes which were to take place began with the acquisition, by the Ministry of Munitions, of a site to the south-east of the village, for the manufacture of munitions based on the deposits of anhydrite beneath Billingham and the salt, so essential to the manufacture of chemical products, which was found in large deposits in the salt marshes in the estuary. The original factory was called the 'Synthetic' as it was planned to produce synthetically the nitrogen which was so important to the war effort. In 1919 the organisation was taken over by Brunner Mond & Co, and later, after amalgamation with other chemical manufacturers, ICI was 'born' in 1926. Billingham has never been the same since!

Of course, it brought great prosperity to Billingham, with hundreds of workers coming from all parts of the British Isles. The way of life of the villagers changed radically. They were no longer farm workers, the occupations of the people were mostly geared to the chemical factory – chemists, engineers, office workers and hundreds of general labourers. Much of the farmland was swallowed up for building workers' houses. However, within 13 years of the formation of ICI England was at war again, and further development was halted.

After the Second World War, the real development of Billingham began with the building of the new town centre, which at that time was quite unique in its design. It was in the 1960s that Billingham became an established venue for a Folklore Festival and by 1967 the town was host to one of the three largest folklore festivals in Europe. Every August, the people of Billingham open their hearts as well as their homes to groups from places as distant as China, Peru, New Zealand and Spain. The new town centre is alive with the sounds of singing and dancing and the colours of the beautiful national costumes of the performers.

In spite of the phenomenal growth of Billingham, it is possible to recapture for a little while that peaceful timeless atmosphere of long ago. Most of the old dwellings around the green have been replaced with more up-to-date houses, but the green is still there and St Cuthbert's church with its Saxon connections. How pleasant it is to take a short break from the bustle of industrial Billingham, and to make a mental journey back through time to 'how it used to be'.

Boosbeck ❧

Boosbeck appears on very early maps simply as the Boos Beck (or Goose Beck on some 16th/17th century versions). There was no hamlet, just a stream flowing through the valley, and a few well scattered farmsteads. The name means 'cow shed by a stream', and well describes the area right up until the late 19th century, when the ironstone mining village was built on high ground to the east.

Boosbeck and Margrove Park lie in a hollow in the hills. At the end of the last Ice Age the whole area was a great melt-water lake. The ironstone seam here dips down into a saucer-shaped depression and it is covered by a waterproof layer of jet and alum shale. In this hollow 'a great underground lake' was trapped, covered by a thick layer of porous sandstone.

When Stevenson, Jacques & Co tried to sink a deep shaft, to tap the seam here, they struck this lake. In February 1886 'a huge spout of water suddenly shot into the air'. The speed and force of the flood-water was far more than the early pumping gear could contain. The shaft was abandoned. Having been tapped, the waters seem to have drained away gradually, probably into the surrounding countryside and via nearby working mines. A few years later Bolckow, Vaughan & Co leased the land from the Skelton Castle estate and tried again. They were more successful. Their mine was worked for many years, but it frequently suffered from flooding and associated problems. Not until it was modernised, and a new entrance shaft sunk by Dorman Long in 1929, did the mine become really profitable. Four hundred and fifty men were employed there in 1945.

When the mining village was being built, Mr J. T. Wharton of Skelton Castle donated land for a parish church, and St Aidan's was dedicated in 1901. Until then the area had been part of the ecclesiastical parish of Skelton.

By far the oldest buildings are at Holly Well Farm, on the junction of the Lingdale and Margrove Park roads. For many centuries a habitation has been shown at this spot on successive maps. In the 13th century it appears at Holly Keld Cote (Keld meaning stream or well). Of the 19th century village some of the earliest homes would have been the row of terraced cottages, built near the church, to house the brick workers. The Carrs Tilery and Brickworks were opened in 1867, half a mile south of the new village. Remains of the clay pit and quarry can be seen today, to the left of the road.

At the turn of the century Boosbeck also boasted a Methodist chapel, a railway station, a picture theatre, an institute and a school. The station served the first four miles of track on what eventually became the Guisborough–Whitby line. A report in the *Whitby Gazette* dated 3rd November 1878 tells of a near tragedy. Shallow workings in the Skelton Park Mine collapsed due to flooding. The sudden subsidence left 40 ft of the up and the down railway line suspended in mid-air. The noise was heard by the signalman, and by platelayers working just outside the station. Just in time they managed to stop an on-coming train carrying some 30 passengers, men, women and children.

The railway line is now closed and the station site is used for industrial purposes; the picture theatre has gone; the old school is now a nursing home, but the village is far from dying. A new school has been built, also serving the surrounding villages. Houses are going up again to supplement the old terraced cottages, and the Lockwood Beck Parish Council is determined to bring a new lease of life to the area.

Boosbeck stands to the north of the tiny hamlets of Margrove Park, the Charltons and Slapewath, overlooking the valley with its beautifully wooded hillsides. The old village school at Margrove Park houses the Heritage Centre. Here a permanent display, as well as changing exhibitions, reflect

18

the past, present and sometimes future plans for the region. A nearby caravan park, and an old inn at Slapewath, which offers good food and accommodation, all add to the tourist potential. It is hoped that more holidaymakers will turn off the busy Guisborough–Whitby road and seek out this hidden valley.

Boulby 🦋

Boulby today is famous for its potash mine. A borehole was sunk just before the Second World War and was the first recorded find of potash in England. The site is just inside the Yorkshire National Park and every endeavour is made to protect the environment. The salt residue is normally pumped out to sea, but in extremely cold weather they can increase production to cope with the demand from the authorities for salt to keep the roads open.

The Domesday Book has the first recorded use of the name Bollebi, meaning Bolli's Farm. Boulby was divided into two holdings, one of a carucate worth eight shillings, the other of two carucates, which had been laid waste. Boulby was a very small hamlet and for centuries for administrative purposes was linked with other nearby settlements. It is not until the 13th century that dwelling places are mentioned at Boulby. Boulby is sometimes mentioned as Easington-cum-Boulby.

Feudal aid in the 14th century links Boulby with Glapphowe. Location of this site has not been defined. Fifteenth century records show that there were several tenants at Boulby. The static pattern of life at Boulby did not change until the late 1500s. George Conyers owned the manor of Easington, and he kept a dwelling house at Boulby. The Conyers also owned the valuable alum workings on the coast. They sold the property at Boulby and by the 19th century it was in the hands of the Whartons. The manor house was now only a farmhouse, but the lintel over the door was carved with the escutcheons and arms of the Conyers. The farm was still in use in 1838, but on the Ordnance Survey map of 1856 Boulby Hall is marked as an antiquity. The settlement was finally abandoned at the beginning of ironstone mining in 1875.

The archaeologists have discovered that the earliest settlement had stone-built dwellings, with the exception of one which was made of wood; this is fairly typical of a small manorial medieval complex. The next development shows that two large buildings had been added. Boulby has never been more than a hamlet, and in the latter days of its life was only a farmstead.

Brotton ✺

Before the Conquest, Brotton (Broctune) belonged to Uctred, a Danish Earl. When local landowners were deprived of their estates, Brotton was given to the Earl of Mortain, half brother to William I. The Earl of Mortain gave Brotton to one of his retainers, Richard de Sundeval. Later it was added to the many manors of Robert de Brus.

There is evidence that ancient man settled in this area about 2,000 BC. A coffin made out of a hollowed-out oak tree trunk containing the skeleton of a Bronze Age man, was found on Howe Hill. A second barrow with cremated remains in an urn, with an accompanying food urn, was found on the summit of Warsett Hill.

In the late 14th century the Black Death reduced the population of Brotton, and Cleveland as a whole, by two thirds. There was a village green and the manor house stood

20

at the north-west corner. There was a pinfold where stray animals were kept until they were redeemed by their owners. The lane to the south led to Kilton Castle. The church at Brotton, like so many others in Cleveland, was given to Guisborough Priory. Later it became the parochial chapelry subject to Skelton and comprised Kilton, Carling Howe and Skinningrove.

In the 18th century the old church was replaced by a new one on the same site. A hundred years later another new church was built and dedicated to St Margaret. A Miss Jackson paid £5,000 for the building of this church, a fine example of Victorian Gothic architecture. When St Margaret's was built the old church became the mortuary chapel. This chapel was restored and cleaned in 1901 but was demolished later. When the workmen removed some large flagstones near to where the altar had stood they discovered a tunnel, which had been bricked up some time in the past.

Brotton, like many other Cleveland villages, was caught up in the iron ore rush (that doesn't sound as romantic as a gold rush but it was in many ways just as important). In 1866 the population was 330 and ten years later it had increased eightfold to 2,672. This influx of people from all over the country made hospitality a necessity. Brottonians are noted even today for welcoming strangers into their midst. At the time of the mining boom Brotton village green was built over. There is now only one 17th century cottage remaining.

The mineshafts at Brotton were among the few to be run under lease to a Mr Morrison. He sold the ore on contract. There were two mineshafts about 150 ft deep. In the early days of mining, candlelight was the only means of illumination. If the wind was a strong south-westerly it blew straight into the shafts and blew the candles out. In some places these mineshafts were very close to the surface, and when the miners were blasting, cottages nearby suffered broken windows and china was vibrated off the shelves. The miners on the other hand could hear the noise and feel the vibration of the trains as they passed overhead. The mines despatched 34 ore trains of 22 trucks every day. Each truck contained ten tons of ore. The dangerous nature of the work made the provision of medical care absolutely necessary.

Bell Brothers built a 17-bed hospital in 1874, staffed voluntarily by the Sisters of the Holy Rood community from Middlesbrough. At first Bell Bros totally supported the venture, but when it was expanded to include the ironworks at Skinningrove the workers contributed a penny a week for its upkeep. The local population supported it in many ways, farmers and others would send eggs, rabbits, and any other produce they could spare. Early ambulances were like costermonger's barrows and the patients were pushed to the hospital, later horse-drawn vehicles were used.

When it became apparent that a school was needed, Miss Jackson once again displayed her generosity and donated the land and £150 towards the building. St Margaret's Church of England school for 100 pupils was opened in 1866.

During the 1920s when the depression was gaining momentum and the demand for iron ore was in decline, each morning the miners listened for the mine hooter. If it sounded once there was work that day. If it sounded twice they could stay in bed. Money was very short at this time and Squire Wharton had his forester mark certain trees on his land, and the villagers could go along and fell these to use as fuel on their home fires.

Brotton today is a mixed society. The village is a little dour in appearance but the villagers have a kindly heart. There are some new developments. Employment is at British Steel at Skinningrove and other industries in the Tees valley.

Carlton ✣

The origin of the village of Carlton lies in the remote past. The pattern of the village was probably determined in the 11th or 12th century when estate reorganisation was commenced.

It is part of the ecclesiastical parish of Redmarshall which came under the auspices of the Bishop of Durham, and is situated north of the river Tees, about five miles to the west of Stockton-on-Tees. Until boundary reorganisation in 1974 it was part of the county of Durham. It is 160 ft above sea level, and was essentially a small agricultural village, the farmhouses and cottages built on either side of the main village street, probably an old drovers road, with a slow flowing stream running alongside the south of the settlement.

In 1200 Bishop Pudsey of Durham caused a survey (the earliest on record) to be made of all his possessions. This included Carlton, in which there were 23 farmers and a miller. William, son of Orm of Carlton, had to come to the great chase of the Lord Bishop with one greyhound whenever required. Towards the end of the 14th century there were 124 residents and at that time tenants had a common bakehouse, the lease being two shillings paid to the Bishop.

Life in Carlton until the beginning of the 20th century was very different and much harder than that enjoyed by residents today. The only water supply was from the village pump, situated in the centre of the village; piped water was installed about 1895, although the village pump was still in general use many years later.

Transport and travel was by foot or horsepower until the introduction of the railway to the east of the village, when a railway station (originally named Carlton station) was constructed in about 1850. Once the Carlton station was operating it became the local centre of industry, with goods trains, chemical works, coal depot and very welcome passenger trains. Houses and cottages were built for the workers, many of whom were housed in the village, and this increased the population considerably at this time. Farmers used the railway regularly to send their milk to the dairies in the town; cows were milked, milk cooled and measured into churns and transported by horsepower to catch a train due before 7 am so that it could be delivered at its destination fresh for breakfast.

A bus service was introduced in the 1920s. Initially the bus ran only twice a week, market day and Saturday, but this has now developed into an hourly service every weekday.

Many changes in the way of life in Carlton have taken place in recent years, and are often described as 'before' or 'after' the war (1939/45). During the 19th century 'travelling men' with stallions used to visit the village to service the mares owned by local farmers. As the horse was the predominant method of transport of the day, the travelling men would stay overnight at a farm in the village before going on to the next stop. The horse and cart mode of travel gradually gave way to the motor vehicle during the 20th century, and today the village is troubled with increasing traffic, some exceeding the 30 mph speed limit which was introduced in 1978.

Up until the advent of the 'combine', a steam thrashing machine travelled the area spending a day at each farm thrashing the corn. Thrashing Day was a big event on the farms, about 20 local men and women worked on the thrasher, from about 6 am until dark. The farmer's wife had a busy day starting with breakfast (traditional), ten o'clocks, dinner (roast beef) and three o'clocks, plenty of good food for such hard work.

Before the war there were many natural landmarks, which have now sadly disappeared. There were well used footpaths around the village, about five duck ponds, orchards, trees and hedgerows. Progress meant that roads had to be widened and old property demolished, but village greens are still very pleasantly established, lately enhanced by bulbs planted by residents and regularly maintained by the Stockton Borough Council.

Services are held each Sunday in the Methodist chapel, built in 1871, which stands in a prominent position at the east end of the village at the junction of the roads leading to Stockton and Thorpe Thewles.

A public house, the Smith's Arms, stands well in the centre of the village, built in about 1900 (by Irish labourers lodged in the village) to replace an ancient inn nearby. The South Durham Hunt partake of the 'Stirrup Cup' and meet here twice in the season. The blacksmith's shop, now the new lounge, situated next to the pub was a centre of activity in the village, gossip was exchanged, the world put right and horses shoed, a very warm place to be on a cold day.

Although the village was originally a farming community with associated small industries, 'before the war' there were five working traditional farms and now only one such farm is left.

Children from the village attended the local church school at Redmarshall until it was closed in 1966, when a new primary school was built at Bishopton.

In 1928, a group of ladies, headed by the stationmaster's wife, held a meeting to form a Women's Institute. Many functions were held to raise money to build the hall which was completed in 1936, and which has been a great asset to both the Women's Institute and the local community.

The first post office to be established was in 1933, when a room in a local cottage was converted for this use. The arrival of the public telephone was much later.

There is local knowledge of a small shop at Middle Farm at the beginning of the century, and later at what is now called Glenesk Cottage. Travelling salesmen were the order of the day, until the advent of the motor car. Fruit and fish men and butchers came weekly by horse and cart.

There is no record of any serious crime in the parish, probably that is why there was never any resident village 'bobby'. Under new police regulations Carlton is now served by a community policeman.

Christmas Eve 1936 was a momentous day for Carlton. The electricity was switched on and things were never the same again, candles and oil lamps were thrown away. Street lighting was installed in 1963.

A fairly recent addition is the playing field, established in 1975, and donated to the parish by the late Mr Fred Hall, a local farmer, whose antecedents can be traced back to the 18th century in the area.

In the original village there are many old properties, including some which are 'listed'. In recent years new residential development has taken place which has dramatically increased the population. The situation of the rural village of Carlton, so near to the large industrial area of Teesside, has made it a convenient and desirable residential district.

Carlton was for many years part of the Rural District of Stockton-on-Tees which was later amalgamated into the new County of Cleveland. The population in 1841 was 157, and 150 years later is about 550. A strong community spirit still prevails, primarily through the efforts of the Women's Institute, the church and the chapel.

Charlton ꧁

Charlton, known locally as Charltons, consists of two rows of terraced houses at the foot of Birk Brow – the moor road to Whitby. The village was developed due to ironstone

Victorian Spa Wood Viaduct at Charlton in the 1860s

mining in the 1860s and within a one mile radius there were three mines, Spawood (Sporwood) on its doorstep being of most interest to Charltons. These mines and drifts brought a network of railway bridges and an eleven-arched viaduct – fine examples of Victorian skills. The community was very close. The houses were built by T. Charlton, mine owner of Westgate, Guisborough.

Birk Brow was a hazardous road and even now needs treating with respect in bad weather, although it has been altered. The road has given rise to present day village occupations, with two garages, two repair yards and a breaker's yard. In the 1920s and 1930s when cars first came on the road, lads used to sit at the awkward bends and when cars stalled 'they earned a copper or two' by helping to push them up the steep hill.

The railway came in 1861, and enabled the ore to be transported to the furnaces of Stockton and Middlesbrough. Men were employed from all round the area and as lead mines were closing in Teesdale, these miners transferred to Cleveland.

The village itself consists of two straight terraces of houses with six tall houses at the front which once housed overseers and deputies; it has one corner shop. Rents in the 1920s were three shillings and fourpence per week, when each yarded house had an allotment and each house kept a pig and killed their own. Food was plentiful and 'not one piece of the pig was wasted'.

The houses were bought by Dorman & Long, when they became mine owners. In 1962–1970 they were sold to sitting tenants for £100 each. Today there are only eight council houses, the others being owner-occupied. There was a third row of houses – Reading Room Row was demolished because of mine subsidence.

At the back of the houses to the right is the old stable, reminiscent of drovers' road stables, which housed the horses from Sporwood Mine. This is now a vehicle repair yard. Adjoining it is Noddings Abattoir, at one time a tannery but now dealing with animals and animal feedstuffs.

Charltons is now a quiet village with an independent breed of people. In the 1920s and 1930s it was a hive of activity. There was a butcher's shop on the road to Hollins Farm, a haberdashery in someone's sitting room, a baker's and a sweet shop. There was also a fish shop at which 'Nelly-one-pan' operated – she only ever used one pan for fish and chips. Nicknames are prevalent and pertinent in this area. Norman Broadley made bikes out of scrap, painted them black and sold them for six shillings. The village had a brass band, football team and a cricket team. The wooden Miner's Institute maintained by Dorman & Long had a library, reading room and billiards, and a hall for dancing and meetings. The reading room had been on the end of the street which had to be destroyed. Underneath there were miners' baths. They walked from all round the area to dances played for by a pianist, and many people still go dancing, especially the 60 to 70 year olds. The Institute was burned down in the 1970s but a new community hall is still well used and at the moment houses the Lockwood Beck Textile Map of five villages which has been made in the community.

The water supply to Charltons came from a spring on the hill to three 'taps' at the back of each street. It was 1952 before houses were given running water and flush toilets. The spring was used until the 1960s when Scaling Dam was opened. Water was collected daily for each house. On Friday nights the residents took their soap and towels down the three streets to queue in the brick waiting room for their turn in one of the three baths provided. There was an old iron bellied stove for heating the water. Sometimes they waited for hours to bath and if they filled the bath too full they were in trouble because people had to wait even longer for the water to heat again. The charge was three pence per bath and two children had to share a bath of water. 'The ladies went in before the men from the mine came home'. Unfortunately at that time if a man lost his job then he lost his home as well.

Transport was with Readmans and John Dobson, who ran brakes with horses to Guisborough and surrounding villages. When brakes with two horses went up Birk Brow then people got out and walked. John Dobson then progressed to buses – the rattling Charltonians which did not appear to run on time. Today the village has a firm of coaches, Best Way Travel, and are served by the local bus.

Among the older people there can still be heard the old dialect, which is nearly Old English with even an odd Saxon word. It is spoken with phonetic pronunciation and a diphthong. A pity this is being lost as it is from the old Cleveland.

Coatham 🌿

In 1068 two Northern earls raised a rebellion against the Norman invaders. William marched north at the head of his army to quash this rebellion; folklore suggests that the English rebels made their last stand on Coatham Marshes, but were soon defeated.

Marmaduke de Thweng applied for and got a licence from Henry III for a market and fair at Coatham in 1257. Coatham has also had saltworks for over 600 years. Surprisingly Coatham had a viable small port, comprised of six to eight inlets, and the cargo was unloaded directly onto the beach. Coal ships called at this port and the monks transported the coal and other goods overland to various destinations.

There are references to a chapel among the sandbanks. Its location is not stated, but it probably stood near to Marsh House Farm. The chapel was possibly used as the burial place for drowned mariners.

Coatham was part of the estate belonging to the Turner family of Kirkleatham Hall. Sir William Turner employed John Agar, a yeoman farmer living at Coatham East, to collect the dues for anchorage, groundage, and beaconage. His job also involved recording the movement of shipping and cargoes. This position was terminated in 1808 when the Tees Navigation Company was created by an Act of Parliament.

The first census of 1801, when Coatham was still in the parish of Kirkleatham, showed that the population was 680. By 1821 the population was much the same, 686. Although there was some agriculture in the area, the sea and its accompanying activities was the mainstay of the community. With the decline of the port Coatham became a quiet watering place. Amusements were simple, with visitors and locals content with the sand and a gentle walk along the front, and the occasional game of cards in the evening. A whole house could be rented for two to five guineas a week. During the season the local paper printed a list of notable people arriving and departing from Coatham and where they stayed.

The Turner family provided a free school for the education of 50 poor children. Twelve of these children were given a new suit of clothes each year.

The 1851 census shows that there were 75 houses along Coatham High Street and another four houses near to Marsh House Farm. The first new houses were built in Victoria Terrace. Coatham had a railway station which was called Redcar Station. Behind this stood Railway Terrace, a group of four white brick houses to accommodate the railway workers. When the station was closed these houses were dismantled brick by brick and rebuilt at Kirkleatham where they still stand.

At the corner of West Dyke Lane and Milbank Terrace stood Green House, and nearby was the site of Coatham windmill and millhouse. Today the United Reformed church stands on this site. The community had grown sufficiently by 1854 to support its own church. Christ church was built under the patronage of Mrs Newcomen of Kirkleatham Hall, who was also responsible for the vicar's stipend. The church stood isolated to the north of the village and south of the Cleveland Hills. Christ church became known as the 'Church in the Fields'. Mrs Newcomen was also the patron of the library and reading room, and the village school.

The most famous school in Coatham was Sir William Turner's grammar school. Originating at Kirkleatham, the Charity Commissioners ordered that it had to be resited, and it was rebuilt in Coatham Road in 1869. A century later it was resited again in Corporation Road. The name is still preserved in the academic world by Sir William Turner's Sixth Form College on Redcar Lane.

Reverend John Postlethwaite, the first vicar of Christ Church, bought a piece of land from Mrs Newcomen in 1860 upon which was built Coatham Convalescence Home. Constructed of red brick it had magnificent views across Coatham Bay towards the Tees estuary and along the coast to Marske. The patients were 'poor respectable persons'. Redcar Borough Council bought the building after the Second World War, and demolished it. This is where the leisure centre now stands. Coatham was untouched by industrialisation until the Coatham Iron Works was established in 1873.

Coatham had its own pier in 1875. It had two pavilions, the central one for band concerts and the one near the entrance was the roller skating rink. Dogged by misfortune the pier was almost completely wrecked by the barque *Binger*. It is surprising that the *Binger* caused such havoc. She first sprang a leak near the Dogger Bank more than 100 miles to the south. At the mercy of tides and winds she came to rest at Coatham. Crashing over Saltscar Rocks, her masts snapped, the crippled boat broke through Coatham Pier, leaving a gap 100 yards wide. Two of the 15 crew were very lucky to survive. Coatham Pier Company could not afford to have the pier repaired and it quickly became dilapidated.

There was a great deal of rivalry between Coatham and Redcar. A mobile bandstand was used between the two resorts until a permanent stand was built facing the park. This park was known locally as 'Titty Bottle Park', because nannies of the more wealthy residents pushed their charges around the park for their daily airing.

The decision to unite Coatham with Redcar was proposed by Kirkleatham in 1896. It was bitterly opposed by Redcar until the very end. The proposal was that Kirkleatham,

Yearby and Dunsdale were to revert to the control of Guisborough Rural Sanitary Authority, and Coatham was to unite with Redcar. This union was enacted on 1st March 1899.

Coatham today is overwhelmed by Redcar and its existence as a separate entity is almost ignored.

Coulby Newham ❧

This new village to the east of Hemlington is a thriving modern community. A smart covered shopping precinct with a variety of shops adjoins a multi-purpose sports complex, the Rainbow Centre. The Royal Shakespeare Touring Company have played here, and television's popular programme *The Antiques Roadshow* stopped here.

The Roman Catholic community have built a large cathedral here, modern in design it replaces the former cathedral in Middlesbrough. The cathedral was blessed at its opening by Archbishop Basil Hume of Westminster.

The local authorities have retained one of the farms, and it is called Coulby Newham Leisure Farm. It is open to the public for a small fee, and local school parties make use of it for educational purposes.

Cowpen Bewley ❧

Cowpen Bewley is pronounced 'Coopen Bewley'. Cowpen most probably comes from the Scandinavian 'kuppa', a bowl-shaped vessel – could this be a salt-making vat? Bewley is a derivation of Beaulieu, a name added by the Benedictine monks.

Cowpen Bewley is an example of a planned medieval

village, with common grazing land in the centre. Today this grazing land is the village green and looked upon as a visual and useful amenity, but in medieval times the lord of the manor would make sure that the villagers had easy access to grazing land for their own livestock. After all, part of this livestock was the lord's tithe money and it was to his benefit as well. The village had fallow land for crops immediately behind the cottages. Cowpen Bewley also had a third harvest, salt. The villagers of Cowpen Bewley paid rent to the Prior of Durham for the privilege of producing salt from the surrounding salt marshes.

The Three Horseshoes public house at Cowpen Bewley was in the same family for four generations, 120 years. The pub was the centre of village life. At one time they brewed their own beer on the premises. The Three Horseshoes was the venue for the village Autumn Feast (Harvest Festival) when a feast was prepared on the evening after a day of horse racing, foot racing, and other competitions. After the feast they held a dance in a large upstairs room. When the railway was under construction, a temporary halt was created near to the pub. A hoot on the train's whistle warned the landlady that they were coming and the doors were opened in readiness for the railway navvies to rush in to have their mid-day meal and beer.

Early in the 20th century the Friendly Club, the pride of Cowpen, had its headquarters in the Three Horseshoes. The members paid one shilling and threepence a fortnight. One shilling was their 'sub' and threepence they had to spend in the pub. This club enabled members who were off work because of sickness to draw ten shillings a week after a certificate from a doctor was produced, a great help in the days before the welfare state.

Despite Cowpen Bewley's close proximity to the petro-chemical industry, it has never been extended and made into a dormitory place for the workforce of Teesside. The village was owned by the Priors of Durham until it was sold to ICI earlier this century. It is surprising that Cowpen Bewley has escaped the worst of the pollution that has blighted other villages in this area. Cowpen Bewley today is still a picture of rural simplicity and calm.

Dalton Piercy

To many people Dalton Piercy is not a 'proper' village since it has no church, no school and no pub. Although it is only three miles from Hartlepool and less than one mile from the A19 trunk road the village is relatively isolated with public transport being limited to four buses per day into town. A school bus is provided by the Local Education Authority to transport primary school children to the Church of England school in the neighbouring village of Elwick. This service was only introduced in 1960; before then the children had to walk across the fields. Older children attend comprehensive schools in Hartlepool or travel to private schools in other parts of the county.

Originally called Dalton – 'the enclosed homestead in the valley' – the village was once part of the manor of Hart which was granted to Robert de Brus by William the Conqueror. It was later transferred to the Balliol family and the 'Piercy' was added to its name in the 13th century when Ellen, daughter of Ingram de Balliol married William de Percy, Duke of Northumberland, and brought him the village as part of her dowry. There is no trace of the original homestead. The oldest dwellings appear to be Priory and College Farms which both have buildings which may date from the 17th century. There are a few 18th century buildings and some fine Victorian houses, the most outstanding being 'The Villa' which is at the end of a terrace on the south side of the green. This was originally called Wake Villa after its builder Thomas Wake. From 1906 to 1914 it was used as a home for crippled children.

Until quite recently the village green was a perfect example of a medieval 'two-row' form and was gated at each end to keep in the cattle. The village pump, once the focal meeting point of the village, can still be seen on the green but it has not been used since mains water was installed in the 1940s. At the western end of the green the previously silted-up pond has been reinstated by the parish council. Unfortunately Dalton's village green, unlike that of Elwick, has not been protected by a conservation order and much modern building has detracted from its character.

Since 1972 the village has expanded considerably with the building of 'executive-type' housing to the west and north of the green. Consequently most of the present population are relative newcomers to the area with 'middle-class' occupations in Hartlepool or Teesside. The family which can claim the longest association with Dalton Piercy are the Jobsons of Manor Farm, which has been owned by their family since the early 1800s. In 1848 Joseph Jobson, grandfather of the present farmer, came from Benknowle Farm at Elwick at the age of 16 to take over from a maiden aunt and was there until he died at the age of 90.

The village is linked to Elwick, one mile to the north, by an ancient bridleway – now used only as a footpath – and other public rights of way lead over the fields to Hartlepool. One of these footpaths follows the course of the Char beck which flows across the eastern end of the green into a long stretch of meadow known locally as the 'Batts'. This was once a popular picnic spot for families from Hartlepool who brought their children into the countryside at weekends and during school holidays. In the 1940s a tea-shop and sweet shop at the end of the green provided welcome refreshments after the walk. Picnicking was banned some years ago because of wilful damage caused by trespassers but the footpath is still well used, being part of a circular route much favoured by the organisers of sponsored walks.

A large area of land to the north of the village is owned by the Hartlepool Water Authority who have a pumping station there. Part of this land, a heavily wooded area known as the 'Howls' which is a favourite playground for village children, was sold to the Cleveland Conservation Trust in 1990 for a nominal fee of £1 so that it can be managed as a nature reserve. An ancient spring in the woods was refurbished by villagers to mark the Queen's Silver Jubilee in 1977 but sadly it is once again out of use due to vandalism.

The village appears never to have had a pub, although Priory Farm was once a brewery. The old Red Lion pub, now replaced by the modern Dalton Travel Lodge, was some way from the village on the opposite side of the A19 road. Dalton does not have its own church as the village is part of the sprawling parish of Elwick Hall whose church is on the outskirts of Elwick village. A Methodist chapel did exist from 1884–1910 in a building known as 'Elt's House' after a former occupant named Eltie Metcalfe. A Mrs Stokell, who ran a market garden in the village with her husband, used to lay out the dead and arrange funerals. She was also the village midwife! Another Mr & Mrs Stokell also owned a market garden, at Rose Cottage. Their surplus produce which could not be sold in the village was carried in baskets by Mrs Stokell over the fields to Hartlepool where Mr T. Stokell Junior had a market stall on Saturday mornings. There has been no shop in the village since the last one was destroyed by fire in the early 1980s. Milk and newspapers are delivered daily and a travelling butcher calls once a week, as does the mobile library, but for all their other needs the residents must go to the village post office in Elwick or travel into town.

With such a lack of public amenities villagers have to look elsewhere for their entertainment or make their own. In the 1950s an ex-army hut was bought to serve as a village hall. Situated to the south of the green, behind Priory Farm, it is still used for a variety of activities arranged by the village hall committee and the parish council, such as keep-fit classes, a weekly coffee morning, musical evenings and quiz nights. At Three Gates, a small group of dwellings approximately quarter of a mile to the west of the green, there is a riding school, which as well as being popular with the village children also provides facilities for riding for the disabled. Many residents are keen gardeners and they get the chance to exhibit their flowers and produce at the annual Dalton Piercy Horticultural Show. This is a very popular event, with a wide variety of classes, in which all age groups are encouraged to take part.

Dunsdale ✤

Dunsdale is a relatively modern village, situated on the B1269 between Wilton and Guisborough. It was built to house the influx of miners after iron ore was discovered in the hills to the south of Wilton, and is near to the carriage way of the old Wilton Castle. The locals pronounce Dunsdale as 'Dunzell'.

There were originally only two rows of terraced cottages, and when the mines closed Dunsdale almost became a ghost village. Today, however, it is a thriving community and the old houses have been modernised. Most villagers are employed at British Steel or ICI Wilton.

Eaglescliffe ✒

It is generally acknowledged locally that Eaglescliffe came into existence by accident, and that before 1852 there is no record of such a place.

Tradition has it that when the new Leeds Northern railway line was built in 1852 to replace the old Stockton to Darlington line, after a dispute with the land-owner through whose grounds it ran, a new station was built to replace Preston Junction. It was to bear the name of the nearest village – Egglescliffe, but the signwriter sent to paint the name on the station was given a piece of paper with the name wrongly spelt 'Eaglescliffe'. Why this was not corrected at the time is not explained but the part of the old parishes of Egglescliffe and Preston around the station on both sides of the main road became known as Eaglescliffe and in recent years has far outgrown the small and much older village of Egglescliffe.

Other than the farms which occupied most of the land in the area, the early building in Eaglescliffe was limited to a number of large Victorian terraces and detached houses built in the late 19th century for the more prosperous merchants in the nearby town of Stockton-on-Tees, who were moving up in the world and out of the town. These houses had attic rooms for domestics and many still have the out-buildings which were originally stables for the horses used to transport the family to business and pleasure. Apart from the area around the station these houses mainly followed the main road from Stockton to the ancient market town of Yarm.

The first elementary school, now called Preston Primary, was opened in 1908 to serve the population of the small terraces that were built alongside the railway line. Very little more expansion occurred until after the Second World War when a small council housing estate and a small number of modest private houses were built, all near to the railway station which was still very much the centre of the village and where the shops were located.

In 1962 the local residents got together to raise funds to buy and convert an old Methodist chapel into a community centre. Eaglescliffe village hall is still a very lively and busy centre for many clubs and activities and is run voluntarily by and for the community and is quite self-supporting financially.

Eaglescliffe still has two busy churches, both on the main road among the older housing, and not too many years ago the Roman Catholics in the area held their services in a tiny church in the garden of a house in Albert Road. The church is still there although no longer used as such as the locals are now able to travel to the church in Stockton.

Eaglescliffe also boasts a large independent girls day school, Teesside High School which takes pupils from four to 18 years. This was originally a small prep school in one of the large houses on Yarm Road, run by the two Miss Chalmers and opened about 1940. The oldest and largest houses in the village are in 'The Avenue' opposite Station Road and these were owned by some of the local gentry including Sir Samuel Sadler, and Sir John Harrison who lived at one time in Woodside Hall. During the Second World War most of these houses were taken over for the staff of the giant chemical works at ICI Billingham, presumably to take all non-essential workers away from the dangers of bombing. In the grounds of Woodside Hall were several large huts used by these workers and later in the war these became empty. The expanding school of the Miss Chalmers moved into the huts and then in 1946 the empty Hall was purchased and the school, now known as Cleveland School, began to grow.

In the late 1960s the Miss Chalmers retired and the school amalgamated with another independent girls day school, the

40

Queen Victoria High School in Stockton. Gradually the Hall and the old buildings were demolished and a new modern school built on the site.

Many long time residents of Eaglescliffe, middle-aged as well as elderly, will tell you that they can remember 'when all this was nothing but fields' and the golf course still had sheep grazing on it. And then things began to change.

In the late 1950s, land was bought from several farms to begin the building of a large industrial estate. This was followed by a demand for housing in the area for the 6,000 expected employees of the industries and so more farmland was acquired. The factories were to produce a variety of engineering, building, chemical and food products. Another large employer in the area is the MOD Admiralty depot which has been on the site since 1948.

Within the last 30 years, two large housing estates have been built, far out-stripping in size the old Eaglescliffe. Two new primary schools, a secondary school, shops, health centres, a library and a new community centre have been built to service them. The golf course no longer has sheep on it but it does have a smart new club house.

None of the older buildings in Eaglescliffe seem to have a ghost to boast of. However in August of 1982, stories of a ghost in the Radiographic factory on the industrial estate were circulating. It seems that the apparition, the silhouette of a Victorian gentleman in a white shirt, had first been reported in 1969 when the building was quite new. On this later occasion, four ladies working in the dark room claimed to have had separate encounters with him. In the same area, bus drivers travelling along the Urlay Nook Road which runs past the industrial estate, have reported seeing groups of people 'in Tudor style costume' walking across the road above the present level of the highway. There is no evidence to indicate who these strange figures might be, but the modern road surface is considerably lower than it was in earlier times and this would explain the gap between today's road level and the figures seen by drivers.

Eaglescliffe was originally in County Durham but as a result of county boundary changes in recent years it is now part of the newly created County of Cleveland. The railway station to which it owes its existence is still in operation, albeit now an unmanned stop very much reduced in traffic and importance.

Easington 🦡

Easington existed in Saxon times and evidence remains that there was a Saxon/Danish church. After the sacking of the North by the Norman conquerors, Easington was reduced from an area that had had 35 ploughs, to only one villein and one plough. Very few Englishmen were allowed to own land.

The church of All Saints was rebuilt in Norman times, in 1772, and in 1889. When ironstone mining was at its peak in the area, one of the mineshafts went right under the church. Nearby a tunnel, 993 ft long, was blasted through solid rock to take the Loftus to Whitby railway. There was an arrangement whereby blasting in the mine stopped and the trains were re-timetabled to allow church services to be held in relative peace and quiet.

There was one water mill in 1627, by 1725 there were five, and only two in 1900. A rapidly expanding village, it is a mixture of mining cottages, ancient remains and some modern housing.

Egglescliffe

The parish of Egglescliffe is bounded by Stockton on the north, Long Newton on the north-west, Middleton St George on the west and by the river Tees on the south and east; it occupies an elevated position on the steep northern bank of the river. The village is situated near the first fordable place at low water above the mouth of the Tees, and is at the end of a cul-de-sac (Butts Lane) which leads off the main road between Yarm and Stockton.

Many aspects of the village have been the subject of controversy and interest, none more than the derivation of its name. One of its more recent historians, the Rev A. T. Dingle, a former rector, estimated that there had been at least 40 ways of spelling it, ranging from Eggascliff (1085), up to its current spelling. However, its traditional pronunciation was Egscliffe. But does the first element of the name refer to an ancient Norse personal name (Eggir), a church (Eccles or Egglis), or even an eagle? A golden eagle was apparently shot in the area as late as 5th November 1823.

Like many long established villages, its green had a market cross, stocks and a pinfold for stray cattle; the pinder, who collected the stray animals, was paid by the contributions from the villagers. Nowadays, only part of the base of the cross remains.

The parish church, parts of which date from the 12th century when it appears to have been an aisleless nave, was originally dedicated to St Mary the Virgin, as evidenced by the request to be buried at the church of the Blessed Virgin at Eggescliffe which appeared in the will of Wil. Astley of Aislabie in 1508; however, it is has been dedicated to St John the Baptist since the 17th century. Artefact evidence indicates the existence of a church in pre-Norman times, but the earliest documentary evidence dates from 1085 when Gilli, clerk of Eggascliff, witnessed a contract.

The living was substantial, being worth more than £64 per annum in the reign of Charles I, with the glebe comprising some 140 acres of arable, pasture and meadow land. Fortunately ecclesiastical records are good, and much insight can be gained into the life of clergy and parishioners. With the exception of a gap between 1550 and 1574, christening, marriage and burial register records are complete and relatively detailed, reflecting the interest and conscientiousness of many of the rectors.

Dr Issac Basire, rector from 1636, was a Royalist supporter, and during the Civil War, when Egglescliffe was used as a Royalist military post, he was requested by Colonel Hilton in February 1643 to ensure the raising of Yarm bridge each night (traditionally the north arch was supposed to have been replaced by a drawbridge during this war). Evidence of military action occurs in the burial register entry for 1st February 1643, namely 'A soldier slain here at ye Yarum skirmish'.

For his support of Charles I, including personal chaplaincy, Dr Basire was imprisoned in Stockton Castle, and his property and rents sequestered. He eventually managed to flee the country until the Restoration, leaving his wife and family behind to exist on the sequestrator's allowance of £12 16s 0d per annum.

Although set back from the main road, accessibility of transport was important. The tidal river permitted small boats to be built near the existing Blue Bell inn in the late 18th and early 19th centuries. A wooden bridge across the Tees had existed for 200 years before the reputed financing of a new stone bridge by Bishop Skirlaw in 1400. This afforded access to and from the south, but its maintenance was a constant source of dispute with Yarm. An attempt to replace it with an iron bridge in 1805 ended disastrously the following year when the new bridge collapsed.

The advent in 1830 of the Egglescliffe branch line of the Stockton and Darlington railway generated a considerable distribution of coal from the bridge bank depot to other parts of Cleveland, in panniers carried by horses, donkeys and mules.

Besides blanket and huckaback weaving, farming, fruit orchards and strawberry growing in the village, a chemical works was established at Urlay Nook in 1831, and in 1832 a paper mill was built on the site of earlier corn granaries on the west side of the north end of the bridge. The paper mill was badly damaged by fire in 1846, and although rebuilt, failed to recover its trade and later became a vinegar factory, which was finally demolished in 1972 to permit road improvements.

Apparently there was some form of schooling in the area before 1715, as the death is recorded in the parish register that year of James Galaway, schoolmaster. Certainly, according to Rector John Brewster's records in 1814, there was only a dame school for younger children in the parish; older children attended a National school in Yarm. He financed a Sunday school in Egglescliffe in 1817, but a National school did not open in the village until 1839.

Charitable giving has been a characteristic of the parish. In 1660, William Hall founded a charity from land rents in Yarm worth £6 per annum for equal distribution each year on 10th December between five poor widows in the parish, or if none, fatherless children under 13 years. Ann French bequeathed the income from £100 investment in 1836 for the equal benefit of the poor at Christmas.

And so to the present time, when the village has grown with the development of the St Margaret's estate off Butts Lane, but still retains some of its insularity; still one church, one school and one pub, the Pot and Glass, formerly the Pot and Pipe. But is longevity still a hallmark of the populace?

Certainly the records show that a George Peacock, an agricultural servant from Aislaby in the parish of Eggles-cliffe, was buried at Sadberge on 19th December 1706, aged near 138 years!

Elton 🦚

This relatively small village of approximately 1,400 acres of land is bounded on the north by the parishes of Norton and Redmarshall, on the north-west by Bishopton, on the south-west and south by Longnewton and on the east by Hartburn. Its southern boundary is marked by Coatham beck, down to which the land slopes.

The road down Sandy Leas and Coatham Stob was used by packhorses carrying coal from Ferryhill to South Bank through Yarm over 150 years ago. At that time it had the only crossing across the river Tees, and the field named 'Turnpike Field' suggests the presence of a toll gate to catch traders travelling between Stockton, Darlington and Yarm. The Brick Kiln Field was where whinstone had been extracted, with the clay being dug out to reach this stone used to make bricks. From Quarry Close, sandstone was extracted, and the pond near which Coatham beck runs was part of the old quarry. Many of the farmhouses were built of this stone.

The parish church is a neat stone building in the Gothic style restored in 1841 on the site of the old church, but it still has its original Norman doorway and chancel arch with beakhead decoration. Between the chancel arch and two smaller arches is a brightly painted rood screen, designed by J. N. Comper in 1907, showing pictures of six saints on traceried panels. Within the altar rails is a cross-legged figure of a knight in chain armour, with a lion at his feet and two reclining angels with open books supporting the pillow beneath his head. It is possible the knight is Robert Gower of Coatham Stob.

It is recorded in Elton parish register that Mary Benton, a butcher's wife, died in Elton in 1853 at the age of 117 years. She was even reputed to have been as old as 122 years. Mary became quite famous in her lifetime and attracted much attention from neighbouring parishes and many people came to see her.

The public house, the Sutton Arms, was originally opposite the church; it was moved outside the parish boundary when a law was enforced which forbade public houses to be sited within the parish.

Elton Hall was built on approximately the same site as the old Halls, between 1913–1914. Constructed with the finest materials and workmanship available, it has been stated that it should last for 1,000 years. It is now a residential nursing home. The gardens were constructed on the Dutch style, like the Hall, symmetrical, each half mirroring the other, with trimmed box hedges and topiary work in English yew. In a summer house, long since rotted away, it is reported that William Wordsworth once sat whilst a-courting!

There is a Victorian wall post box which the villagers are very proud of and it is still used for today's mail.

A milestone hidden amongst the hedgerows gives the distances to Stockton and to Darlington.

Elwick 🌿

The tall, graceful outline of Elwick's mid 19th century windmill is a familiar landmark to thousands of motorists who hurtle along the A19 trunk road each day. Less than a quarter of a mile away the muted roar of traffic is barely discernible in the village, which has retained its aura of tranquil rural charm despite modern developments. The long village green, with its classic, medieval 'two-row' form, was designated a conservation area in 1975. Unfortunately this was too late to prevent the demolition of several old cottages, including the former butcher's shop and some with deeds dating back to the 15th century, but the pleasant mixture of old, new and renovated properties around the green helps to give the area its 'picture postcard' appearance. This scene, much favoured by local artists, is enhanced by a number of fine mature trees, planted by villagers in 1897 to commemorate Queen Victoria's Diamond Jubilee.

The medieval village of 'Ellewic' probably derived its name from 'Ella', a common Old English name, and 'wic', a dairy farm. Today three working dairy farms still front the village green. Many farms in the district have been owned by the same family for several generations, the most notable example being Benknowle Farm where there has been a Jobson for over 500 years. Although horse-drawn machinery and vehicles have long since given way to tractors and motor cars the village has a registered farrier. Much of his work is with horses at a number of riding schools which have been established in the area in recent years. An engineering workshop on the outskirts of the village repairs farm machinery but modern farming methods have enabled most farms to be worked by their owners without the need to employ agricultural workers.

Approached by a narrow, winding road leading westward from the green, St Peter's church stands opposite the village, perched on a hill rising steeply from the Char beck valley – a favourite haunt of village children, known locally as 'the ghyll'. Regarded as the village church it officially ministers to the parish of Elwick Hall, a large, sparsely populated area to the south. The building dates from 1190–1200 although

The Spotted Cow Inn, Elwick

Saxon gravemarkers at either side of the chancel arch indicate a much earlier church. The parish's most famous rector was John Cosin (1624–1640). Considered to be something of a religious rebel at that time he spent some years exiled in Paris before returning in 1660 to become the first Bishop of Durham after the Restoration. He continued to take a keen interest in Elwick Hall and it was mainly due to his influence that much restoration work was carried out in the latter part of the 17th century.

Little is known about the pirate buried in the churchyard, not even his name, but mentioned in the parish registers, which begin in 1592, is Oliver Cromwell – 'that monster of nature and bloudy tyrant' – whose Parliamentary forces occupied Elwick in 1644. Another person of some notoriety to be connected with Elwick was Mother Midnight, a local witch who was buried 'over the wall' at Hart in the late 16th century. She reputedly lived at Bee Cottage, so named after another former resident, Johnny Lee, who kept bees and without protective clothing was never stung. The registers contain many names familiar in the village today, which can be traced back through several generations but the majority of the present population are relative newcomers.

Elwick did not truly emerge into the 20th century until after the Second World War for at that time the village was still without mains water or electricity. Since then it has expanded northwards and a new Church of England primary school opened in 1959 to replace the old building beside the church. The most rapid expansion took place in the 1960s and 1970s when major improvements to the A19 made commuting to the industrial and commercial centres of Teesside and County Durham much easier. There was some council house building, particularly for old people, but the small estates tucked discreetly behind the green are mostly 'executive-type' housing so Elwick has become essentially a 'middle-class' community. Many residents are over retirement age but most of the working population consist of local businessmen, professional people or managerial staff.

Village social life still centres around the green. Teenagers congregate around the drinking fountain, built on the site of the former village pump, while young boys play football. The village shop-cum-post office provides a valuable service – and a good place to gossip! For many years, weekly whist drives have been held in the Women's Institute hall – formerly the Methodist chapel built c1867 – which is also used by a playgroup. Young Farmers and over sixties clubs, a keep-fit group and art club. The Women's Institute has been an integral part of village life since its formation in 1910. The village pubs, dating from c1850, have retained their old world charm despite extensive interior alterations. The McOrville, named after a famous 19th century racehorse which was stabled and trained on a local farm, was formerly called the 'Fox and Hounds'. This probably explains why it – and not its older neighbour, the Spotted Cow – provides the traditional stirrup cup for the South Durham Hunt which occasionally meets in the village.

One village tradition which has defied all attempts to ban it, for environmental and safety reasons, is the annual 5th November bonfire which attracts huge crowds of townspeople, but other events are now only memories. The annual Elwick Show, established in 1919, was discontinued after 46 years because of escalating costs. The week-long Village Feast has been replaced by a children's sports day, mainly due to lack of adult helpers, but is occasionally revived for special events such as the Queen's Silver Jubilee.

One of the most interesting people in the village today is retired schoolteacher, Miss Adeline Sample, who is Elwick's oldest resident. Daughter of Edward Sample, village schoolmaster from 1882–1925, she has lived in the same house for over 90 years and vividly recalls her childhood and village life at the beginning of the century. Fiercely independent and still very alert, this remarkable lady has provided a wealth of information and anecdotes for local historians.

Eston 🌿

Eston appears in the Domesday Book as Aston or Eston, which means East Town. It is situated only five miles from the east coast. For centuries it was an agricultural hamlet, farmed by and for the monks of Guisborough Priory. Eston lies at the foot of the Eston Hills, spectacular with a covering of snow in the winter, sunwashed purple with heather in the summer.

Eston Nab, an Iron Age fort, was crowned with a beacon or lighthouse, possibly as early as the Saxon period. Later it was one of a ring of beacons to warn of any advancing enemy along the river Tees. The beacon fell into disrepair and was demolished in 1949. An obelisk has replaced the beacon and a plaque records its history. Eston Nab was also used as a signal station in the early days of the Water Board. The office of this board was in South Bank, the reservoir supplying the water was outside Guisborough on the Moors Road. Each day one man had to record the level of the water in the reservoir. The Nab was just visible from the Water Board office. So the man who had measured the water level had to climb to the top of the Nab and using semaphore flags signalled to the South Bank office, where the message was read by the use of a telescope and the report was duly recorded.

The oldest remaining building in Eston is the blacksmith's shop. This building was in situ before 1870, but records of a smith go back to the 15th century. Eston lost its pastoral peace in 1850 when John Vaughan discovered a rich seam of ironstone in the Eston Hills. Eston changed from an agricultural hamlet to a mining village. The mine opened in January 1850 and stayed in production until September 1949. The population of Eston was 465 in 1851. This soon expanded as miners came from all over the country, and particularly Cornwall, to dig the ironstone for a living. A cluster of cottages built to house these miners was named California, as a tribute to the American Goldrush miners.

The streets of cottages built by Bolckow-Vaughan were two-up, two-down dwellings. These were not demolished until 1970, often against the will of the residents. These cottages were heated by open coal-burning fireplaces. Coal was supplied free and the coal cellars which were under the stairs were filled when the boiler houses at the mines received their quota. The two bedrooms of these cottages accommodated growing families and lodgers too. The water tap, sometimes in the back yard, was often used by several cottagers. Well organised housewives kept a bucket of water in their flagstoned pantries for domestic use. This system lasted well into the post-war period until the law demanded that all water taps for domestic use had to be under cover.

Oil lamps were used until the 1920s, and the mat in front of the fire would be a 'proddy' made from old garment clippings as the family roasted their knees in front of the coal fire. Early to bed, their sleep would be disturbed by night soil men who came and emptied the backyard middens. Then by the knocker-up, usually a disabled ex-miner, who tapped on the bedroom window with his long stick. Alarm clocks were a luxury. While it was still dark the miners climbed the steep hill to the mineshaft, carrying their bait tins and a bottle of cold tea, which was their only refreshment until they got home again. Miners like sailors were very superstitious. If the first person they met was a woman as they went to work, they would often turn around and go home for the day. Injuries were commonplace events in the life of a miner, Bolckow-Vaughan built a hospital for them in 1876.

Many of the miners had allotments near to their cottages where they grew their own vegetables, and fattened a pig or two. When a pig was slaughtered they would often share the meat with those not as fortunate as themselves. There was not a lot of poverty, except for some of the old and the severely injured. The year was usually divided by various church activities. Weddings were events that children looked forward to, the bridal couple had to throw pennies to the waiting children as they left the church. There was the annual miners gala, when miners from East Cleveland joined the Eston miners. The Easter Fair was held on Eston Nab. Children rolled their hard boiled eggs down the hill and 'jarped' them, that is to knock your egg against another one until it cracked.

When the mine closed in 1949 many men went to work in the ICI chemical industry and the gigantic British Steel complex built about a mile from Eston. Protests were made about the remaining countryside being spoilt, but the flares and smoke from these industries are a reminder that men are at work.

Eston village changed in the 1960s and 1970s. The old miners cottages were demolished, and the tenants were rehoused in neat flats and council houses. Today there are three supermarkets and an excellent bus service, but the once busy railway station has long since been demolished and the site built over. At one time the red brick Anglican church was frequented by the gentry, miners were mainly nonconformists, now there is just one congregation. Eston still retains its sense of a village community. A new phase in its history is about to start. In January 1991 the first soil was turned on the Eston Hills to create the world's longest dry ski slope and winter sports complex. The phoenix village is changing again; let us hope it stays a village.

Greatham 🦢

Greatham village is surrounded by giants, to the north and south sprawling towns and to the east huge chemical industries, which provide an iridescent display of lights at night, To the west is the extinct village of Claxton, razed to the ground by Robert de Brus, King of Scotland. The towns and industry provide employment for the people of Greatham.

The Bishop of Durham has owned the village and the surrounding land since the Middle Ages, Bishop Stitchel in 1273 having gained the manor from the Crown. It had been confiscated from Peter de Montford, who had fought against Henry III in defence of the Magna Carta. Bishop Stitchel, who admired Peter de Montford, did not wish to profit from the estate and endowed a charity, the Hospital of God, for elderly priests and poor men. The endowment was the whole

54

Sword Dancing outside the Hospital of God, Greatham

of Greatham manor. The present hospital was rebuilt in 1803 during the mastership of William Egerton, later the Duke of Bridgewater. James Wyatt designed the new hospital and was knighted later for his work on Windsor Castle. The hospital is a sheltered home for the brethren, who must be poor and of good character, bachelors or widowers and under 50 years of age. Other housing is provided for retired clergy. In 1973 the 700th anniversary of the hospital, the first of three groups of almshouses were built within the village.

Twelve trustees direct the charity, and one, the master, must live in the village at the official residence, Greatham Hall. The master is appointed by the Bishop of Durham, and since 1944 has also been the vicar of the parish. At the installation of the vicar/master a square sod is cut from the charity land, and is presented to the master at the gates of the hospital. Walking to the little Georgian chapel where the brethren attend divine service, he lays the turf on the altar signifying that he holds office only in the Lord's service.

One master, an entomologist, accidentally allowed one of his bloodthirsty gnats to escape. It thrived in the local marshes. Villagers became immune, but visitors must beware its nasty bite.

A second hospital was founded in 1761 by Dormer Park-hurst, a master of the Hospital of God. He sought equal care for six, now four, poor widows or spinsters, no younger than 50. Preference was given to candidates from Greatham.

The church has been enlarged several times since it was rebuilt in 1792. The interior has arcading which dates from the reign of Richard the Lionheart, and there is evidence that there has been a church on this site since the 8th century. The church tower rises above the trees and the clock with Westminster chimes welcomes all to the village. Children delight in searching for the mice, carved on the pews, which are the trademark of Thomson of Kilburn, known the world over as the Mouseman. Children always congregate at the church gate waiting for the newlyweds to throw coins, a custom of bygone days when the gates were tied and they had to pay for the children to untie them. Good luck is also encouraged by the sounding of the anvil primed with gunpowder. Harry Proctor, the last blacksmith who died in 1983 aged 96, used to make special brass horseshoes and poker sets as good luck gifts for the bride and groom.

The church is dedicated to St John the Baptist and the great community activity takes place near to his saint's day, Greatham Midsummer Feast. This takes place over several days and includes sports and social activities and is over 500 years old. The maypole dance, mostly performed by adult women, has its origin as a fertility dance. Records show that in the past many of the ladies gave birth before summer returned!

Greatham has several market gardens, but the product for which they are famous is salt. A factory was established in

Victorian times. The salt at 1,000 ft underground was mined until 1970, despite being bombed in 1942. Cerebos and Saxa salt was produced here. The Bisto Kids were born here in 1909. Today other well known products are made here, One-Cal, Capri-Sun, and Atora suet.

In 1940 Winston Churchill landed at Greatham aerodrome on a morale boosting visit to the area. A Spitfire from Greatham was shot down in that year. In the First World War 'Tommy' Bulmer, a soldier, was mentioned in despatches and three times wounded. He returned to Greatham, became a noted amateur sportsman and respected businessman. His Premier Transport Company started with one secondhand bus, refitted at his father's mattress factory. Sappers Corner where his garage was situated was named in memory of his war years with the Royal Engineers.

Noon on Boxing Day is the traditional time for the Greatham Sword Dance performed by six Morris Men, led by a King, Two clowns, Rantom Tom, and True Blue (also called Hector) plus a Doctor are players in the accompanying story. Hector loses his head by the swords of the dancers because he insults their King. Regretting their hasty justice in front of so many witnesses, the Doctor is called. This boastful quack proves his worth by restoring life to Hector with a bottle of strong ale, whereupon the dance continues and the Doctor tries to get his pay.

Greatham, whose name means the 'village on stony ground', is a firm rock whose roots run deep.

Hart ❧

Hart village, which derives its name from 'Heorot', the Old English word for a stag, has a long history for it was an important settlement in Anglo-Saxon times.

At the heart of the village lies the church of St Mary Magdalene, which is believed to have its origins in the late 7th century. Although the first church was probably destroyed by the Vikings, evidence of Anglo-Saxon workmanship can be seen in the stonework of the nave, remains of the Saxon chancel arch with a triangular-headed opening above and a carved Saxon sundial. Two Saxon baluster shafts linking Hart with Jarrow and Monkwearmouth, and fragments of crosses are displayed in the church.

Extensive rebuilding seems to have taken place in the Norman period when the square tower with narrow lancet windows was erected. The large Norman font, cut from one piece of stone, remains in the building but today an ornately carved 15th century font is used for christenings. On an outer wall of the church is a medieval carving of St George, or possibly St Michael, spearing a dragon.

Despite its long history, St Mary's is still a very active church, as witnessed in the years following 1977 when parishioners helped raise the £80,000 needed to carry out major restoration work.

To the west of the church a 14th century wall with a doorway is all that remains of the manor house, reminding one that in the years following the Norman Conquest the manor of Hart was granted to the de Brus family, who in 1129 gave the church at Hart with lands to the Priory at Guisborough. When the de Brus family fell from grace in the 14th century the lands at Hart were given to the Cliffords, who held them until the late 16th century when they were purchased by John, Lord Lumley for £5,350.

In 1770 the village was sold to Sir George Pocock, a distinguished Admiral, for £72,000. By 1830 ownership had been transferred to the Marquis (later Duke) of Cleveland of Raby Castle, who bequeathed it to the Aclom Milbank family. In 1987 the lordship of the manor of Hart was purchased by an American, a Mr Hart.

Hart parish registers, which date back to 1577, show that witchcraft features in the area's history. The first case was that of Helen of Hell, who cleared herself of charges of sorcery. However, in 1582 Alison Lawe was suspected of witchcraft and condemned to stand with a piece of paper advertising her crime on her head in the churches at Hart and Norton and in Durham market place.

Another famous female is the figurehead which decorates an outer wall of the White Hart. She is thought to have come from the *Rising Sun*, one of 60 ships wrecked at Hartlepool during a violent storm in 1861.

Nearby one passes an aged boulder, thought to be a glacial erratic which moved down from the north during the last Ice Age. It was once used as a village meeting place.

Hart has always been a mainly agricultural village, but associated 'industries' also developed. In the 19th century Hart had its own stables, birthplace of several famous race horses, including *Voltaire* and his son *Voltigeur* who won the 1850 Derby and the St Leger. Overlooking the village is the early 19th century stone windmill, last operated in 1915 but now undergoing restoration work, whilst the village smithy has been recreated in the grounds of Hartlepool's museum. The 1861 census returns show that Hart also had joiners, cordwainers, a mason, shoemakers, a tailor and dressmaker.

The school, which opened in 1981, continues the work of a school built by the Duke of Cleveland in 1838 for 40 pupils. It was enlarged by subscription in 1871 and again in 1895.

Hart's charming period houses and farms are complemented by harmonious new estates, for today the village is a popular residential area for commuters from Hartlepool, Cleveland and Co Durham. Since the opening of a bypass in 1981 the village has been relieved of the rumblings of heavy traffic and tranquillity has been restored. Yet Hart's community remains lively. Besides providing a home for the friendly WI meetings, the village hall, which was enlarged and renovated in the early 1980s as a result of local effort, also hosts a variety of leisure activities and the annual Horticultural Show.

Hartburn 🐿

Hartburn is a small village in the parish of Stockton. The earliest account of the village is in the Boldon Book, compiled in 1183. A second survey was taken by Thomas Hatfield, Bishop of Durham in 1317.

William de Hertburn, in the Norman period lived in the original manor house and farmed the surrounding land. His brother farmed the land between Redmarshall and Stillington. With the permission of the Bishop of Durham acting as the agent of the King, William de Hertburn exchanged his manor with Wessington in County Durham. This did not include the church and church lands. William de Hertburn became William de Wessington. Mr Frederick Hill, an antiquarian, believes that William was the ancestor of George Washington. The branch of the Wessington (Washington) family to which George belonged purchased Sulgrave Manor in Northamptonshire. In 1987 a document portraying William de Wessington's (Hertburn) ancestry of George Washington was made and sent to Washington in America.

For hundreds of years ropes used on sailing ships which frequented the river Tees were made at Hartburn. Where they were made, Rope Walk, eventually became Harper Terrace. Mr Allison, who has lived in the village for many years says that one of the cottages which stood near to the manor house had displayed a notice for 'generations'. This board stated 'Beware of man traps'!

In 1711 Hartburn, together with Stockton and Preston, by an Act of Parliament, became a separate parish from Norton.

All Saints' church was at one time the village school, which was founded in 1875. Adjoining the school/church are three cottages, two at the front and one at the back, and they were originally known as 1, 2 and 3 School Cottages. In front of the church is a huge boulder which was used in the past for beating flax. The boulder now bears a brass plaque commemorating the Diamond Jubilee of Queen Victoria.

There is an interesting connection between Hartburn and Arsenal Football Club. In 1886 Jack Humble along with three friends at Woolwich Arsenal asked around to see who would be interested in forming a football club. Fifteen men were prepared to pay sixpence each to set up the club. Jack was born in East Hartburn in 1862. Jack and his elder brother left the depressed North East and walked to London, where they found employment at the Arsenal. Jack Humble was connected with Arsenal Football Club for four decades. He was the last surviving, original workman founder of the club.

Hartburn village has managed to retain much of its character despite the urban development on the fields to the west known as Sunnyside. A very popular place with children for picnics, it also has an abundance of wild flowers. There is still a walk from Hartburn village over the fields to Preston Park and the museum. Hartburn is now protected by a preservation order, and there are several listed buildings including the manor house.

Haverton Hill 🌿

There were no houses between Port Clarence and Haverton Hill until the railway was extended from Simpasture to Port Clarence. Bell Brothers discovered a seam of rock salt four miles wide and five miles long near to their iron foundry at Port Clarence. Haverton Hill was developed to house the immigrant specialist salt workers from Cheshire. The houses, shops and school of Haverton Hill were built around the old hamlet of Belasis, close to Billingham.

The Furness Shipyard was established in 1917 on 85 acres of low lying farmland and marshes. The government subsidised the reclamation of this land which was subject to regular flooding. Over a million tons of material was used to raise the level of the land by 15 ft. A large number of Irish navvies were brought in to do this work. The Furness Company built a model village of 564 homes and a hostel to house the workforce. The hostel was for 500 men and the village incorporated many of the latest ideas for garden village development.

A cement works was set up in 1928 and became a subsidiary of ICI, who built a further chemical producing complex, and the model village of Haverton Hill was soon covered in dust and pollution. Many surviving residents remember Haverton Hill garden village with vivid memories of a halcyon childhood.

'We lived in a Furness house because my father worked there. Several of the roads were named after famous admirals, such as Hawke, Rodney and Drake. The houses were built in a rectangle, with each house having its own backyard and a small garden. In the centre was the land supposedly to be used for allotments. Instead it was used as a play area, and nicknamed the 'Backs'. Many happy days were spent playing games while our mothers stood and chatted. One very severe winter the older boys built an igloo and it didn't melt for days. In the summer, a bottle of water and some jam sandwiches and we were off for a day out. Up Cowpen Lane to Cowpen Bewley, a very small village with just a few cottages and farms, its own school and public house. From here we climbed the stile and walked across the fields to Greatham and there we played in the beck. We had to pass the wooden hut where Granny Fenny lived both going and coming back. This we did very quickly because we were convinced she was a witch. Haverton was ideally situated and near the sea, the country and across the river the town of Middlesbrough.

'Attached to the workers' hostel they built a cinema – the Saturday afternoon house of pleasure. There was a large playing field used by the older lads as a football ground or in summer a cricket pitch. It was also the ground for school sports including inter-schools competitions. The original school, too small for the growing community, was used as a library. It cost a penny a day to attend school; this new school was surrounded by three pubs, known as the top, middle and bottom house.

Haverton also had two clubs, the Working Men's Club and the Empire. The latter had a billiard hall and the young men that frequented it were considered to be the lowest of the low. The billiard players did finance the annual club trip to Seaton Carew. Members were taken by train from Haverton station to Seaton and on that day Haverton Hill was deserted.

'The village was well supplied with shops: Pearson's the fruiterer, Hallmark's the undertakers, 'Bob the Jew's' tailors, the chemist's with its fascinating array of labelled drawers and coloured glass bottles, Amos Hinton's and the CWS (Co-op). Around the corner were even more shops including two butcher's, a bank, and a barber's where we had to go to get our accumulators recharged, absolutely essential to operate a real wireless radio set. Most people grew their own vegetables on the allotments, which had wide pathways running through them. This area, known locally as 'Pigeon Park', also housed many pigeons and nearly as many hens and cockerels. The village did not have any electricity, only gas, and the lamplighter came round each evening with his long pole to light the street lamps. The houses had gas ovens but most people did their baking in the oven to one side of the blackleaded grate. Stevenson's farm supplied our milk which we collected in our own jugs, the farmer's wife having carefully measured the milk with her gill-sized ladle.

'1928 and the depression brought hard times and the shipyard laid off a lot of men. The parish hall was converted into a labour exchange where the unemployed had to sign on every day. The dance floor was ruined by the men's hobnailed boots. Further along the road was St John's church and even farther was the area known as 'Sweet Hills' with its own shops, a garage and nearby Toyes Rolling Mill Foundry. ICI, or as it was known locally 'The Synthetic', was beginning full time operation which helped with employment. Billingham Borough Council was founded and it superseded Haverton Hill Parish Council and set about building a lot more houses for the workers at the 'Synthetic'. They also built an imposing council office. Executive housing had been built on 'Hill 60' by the Furness Company, and opposite was St Hilda's, a subsidiary church of St John's at Haverton Hill. There was also a Methodist chapel. We had a doctor, who also attended emergencies at the various workplaces. To complete the picture there was a post office, police station, coalyard and another bank. The depression declined as industry, increased its output in preparation for the Second World War.

Despite the prosperity, Haverton Hill was degenerating, overwhelmed by the pollution. The fertile allotments no longer produced any crops, the metal framed windows were rusting away, and the dust penetrated every nook and cranny. The RAF took over the hostel during the war for the men who serviced and flew the barrage balloons to protect ICI from enemy air attacks. After the war most people moved out and ICI took over Haverton Hill. Now there are only green fields and markers where the roads were. No longer is pollution allowed to poison the land and most of the original places of employment are defunct. There are some survivors of the Haverton Hill of our youth, one butcher's shop and the pubs.

Hemlington 🦢

The original hamlet of Hemlington lies at the old crossroads of the Stokesley to Stockton road and Gunnergate Lane, which went from Marton village to Stainton. Hemlington hamlet lies within Stainton parish. Small though Hemlington was, it lay at the centre of several well-developed farms, Hemlington Hall, Viewly Hill, and Grange Farm which was located to the south-west of the parish, in the order of Guisborough Priory.

Like many villages and settlements close to the 'infant Hercules', Middlesbrough, Hemlington has seen many changes in the 20th century. Middlesbrough Corporation bought Bell View Farm and Hemlington Grange at the turn of the century for the establishment of an isolation hospital. For those who had to travel from Middlesbrough to visit patients the lack of transport at that time certainly ensured its isolation. The smoke, fire and steam from the Middlesbrough blast furnaces was like a scene from Dante's inferno and easily seen from the hill, a free firework show on most days and nights throughout the year. The hamlet at the crossroads was still little more than a few cottages, plus one newly built bungalow.

In the 1970s change enveloped the hamlet. Until 1968 the parishes of Stainton and Thornton were in the rural district of Stokesley, in the North Riding of Yorkshire. With the formation of the County Borough of Teesside, the Borough Commissioners incorporated Hemlington and other North Riding villages into the new county of Teesside. With the expansion of ICI at Wilton, and the clearance of terraced houses from central Middlesbrough, the need arose for more land to build new houses and the farm sites of Viewly Hill and Hemlington Hall were chosen for the housing estates. The A174, the Parkway, was built to reach the industrial area of Wilton. Access to the Parkway was situated close to the old Hemlington crossroads. Eye witnesses testify that the houses were built in record time. It changed Hemlington completely.

The estate is typical of other 1960–1970 housing developments. Some remarkable features were developed, notably a large lake from a natural dip in the landscape. Hemlington Hall Farm, a fine Georgian farmhouse which stands near the lake, has been imaginatively converted into a community centre. Within this development there is housing for the disabled, recreation and shopping areas, with future plans for allotments and a street market. Hemlington is now bordered by another new development, Coulby Newham.

The story of Hemlington is still developing. The hospital closed in December 1989. The site has been designated as an industrial estate, with reassurances that it will be environmentally friendly.

Hemlington hamlet is hardly recognisable, except for one cottage which was the public house in the 19th century. The landlord at this time had his licence taken away. After a ban of 110 years the licence has been restored and it is now called the Gables. This public house incorporates all the old cottages as the old crossroads. Hopefully destiny will not repeat itself and its licence will survive.

High Clarence
& Port Clarence

High Clarence was really an extension of Haverton Hill, separated only by a small park with a recreation ground behind it which was known as the 'Bendy'. All along Clarence Road on the right-hand side was an embankment for the railway line which ran from Haverton Hill to Port Clarence.

The houses at High Clarence were all terraces named after universities and schools such as Eton, Oxford, Harrow, Cambridge and Rugby, and others were named after trees. They were built by Billingham Council in 1927. Although much of the main shopping was done at Haverton at the larger shops, they had their own smaller ones such as a sub post office-cum-general dealer, a fish and chip shop, a draper's and a homemade bread shop. Old Mr Patterson was a well known character, seen riding around on his bicycle which had a huge basket on the front to hold the loaves of bread he was delivering. Then came the school with its gardens and playing fields at the back. Just past the school there was the Cenotaph which had been built to commemorate all the men who had been killed in the First World War and later the Second World War. There was always a great procession on Remembrance Sunday made up of church choirs, the Mayor and all the Councillors, and the veterans of course. The service was always well attended.

Opposite the Cenotaph in the side of the embankment

there were big double doors which when opened led to the fields which ran alongside the river. There must have been some sort of building here at one time as it is said that this was where they kept the prisoners from the First World War, and that they built the road from Port Clarence to Seaton Carew. When the Second World War started a dug-out was made in the same area to house the air-raid wardens.

We are now entering Port Clarence, which was much older. Here we had St Thomas's Roman Catholic church and school and very near to it was the Royal Hotel. There are lots of street houses here which were built by Bell's Ironworks belonging to Sir Joseph Bell, with allotments at the back to grow their produce. As well as the ironworks there was Anderson's Foundry who built railway equipment.

In the area at the back of the houses of High Clarence and Port Clarence there were many fields, which housed Salt-holme Farm and the salt works with their many derricks which pumped the brine to the surface. A lot of land was reclaimed in the area of the river mouth. They used to tip great slag boulders and waste to stop the sea taking over and in so doing created an area of water which came and went with the tide. It was known as the 'Lido' and lots of the younger people used it for swimming. The 'Saltflats' attracted a lot of waders, great for wild-fowlers. This is now known as Seal Sands and attracts many species of wild birds. On the reclaimed land one of the biggest chemical industries in the world has been built.

In 1906 a decision was made to build a transporter bridge to cross the river Tees from Port Clarence to Middlesbrough and on 4th July 1907 a Bill was passed in Parliament giving authorisation. It was built by Sir William Arrol & Co of Glasgow; the time allowed for completion was 27 months and the cost was £68,026. It was opened on 17th October 1911 by Prince Arthur of Connaught and was acknowledged as a remarkable piece of engineering. It takes two minutes to cross and carries 750 passengers and 600 vehicles a day. It was used a great deal by the people of Haverton Hill, and people from High Clarence used to walk there by way of a sub-way under the embankment. At one time it cost a penny to cross the bridge. Saturday night was a popular time to use the bridge to Middlesbrough because there was always a good market held in Sussex Street. If the bridge happened to break down there was a choice of two evils, you could climb up the side of it, walk across the top and down the other side, or otherwise take the ferry!

Hilton 🌿

Hilton is a small village three and a half miles from Yarm and five miles from Stockton. Until a few years ago it was part of North Yorkshire.

In 1955 the lord of the manor owned the estate; there were about five farms, a few smallholdings, one having a small inn attached, and a row of cottages. The estate was put up for sale, most of the tenants bought their properties, and most of the farms are still run by the same families. There is a small village hall that used to be the village school, and also a very interesting church which has been kept in excellent repair and goes back to the 12th century.

The first lord of the manor was one Adam de Hilton and it is thought he built the church around 1166 in the reign of Henry III. Over the years other owners have changed and repaired parts. The front is 18th century, of primitive stone design with a wooden cover. St Peter's was a chapel of ease to Rudby church but became a separate parish in the 19th century with its own vicarage (now part of the Falcon inn).

The register began in 1698 and the first marriage was recorded in 1754.

In 1989 a milestone project was started. A sculptor carved and erected stones in and around the village boundaries depicting village life and the seasons of the year.

Over the last 30 years modern development has resulted in four small areas of housing – the Old Manor site, Fir Tree Close and two Falcon Walks, which one day may be joined up, making about 150 houses in the village – a pleasant place to live.

Hutton 🌿

Hutton village is beautiful, surrounded on all sides by trees, in a narrow secluded valley about two miles south-west of Guisborough, 500 ft above sea level.

Ironstone mining was begun here in about 1853 by Oliver Davidson (in what is sometimes called Codhill mine) and the village came into being to house the workers of the mine. The census of 1861 shows a settlement called Thomas Street, believed to have been called after Mr Thomas, a local landowner, and in 1871 the village was recorded as Thomas Town. A stream rising from above the village ran down to Tocketts Mill some ten miles away. The stream now runs into a culvert under the road, but in front of the gatehouse can still be seen the arch of the bridge which used to span the stream.

A small seam of jet found above the ironstone working was mined from about the 1840s to the 1880s around the village.

St Andrew's mission was built in 1856 by Sir Joseph Pease (a Quaker) as a place of worship for his estate workers and the ironstone miners who lived in the village. The building ceased to be used for services early in the 1970s as it was by then in a bad state of repair. One or two worshippers plus the vicar falling through the floor boards may have hastened its closure! The property is now a private house.

A railway was built to carry the ore down the line to Guisborough, and the first station was built in the year 1861. In 1864 the station was built at Hutton Gate. A magnificent red brick mansion house, Hutton Hall, was built by Sir Joseph Pease in about 1867, with a large stable block and gatehouse, and extensive landscaped gardens. In the large number of greenhouses on the estate grew bananas, peaches, nectarines, grapes and apples. There was even a large boating lake. The house belonged to the Pease family until it was sold to a Mr Pickering, a shipowner, in 1902, and later in the 1930s it was sold to the owners of the Middlesbrough estates. The Hall can be seen from the road to Hutton village and one can imagine how beautiful it was in its heyday. Sadly now the building is no longer one private house, but is split into flats. The stable block to the left of the Hall is delapidated and the gatehouse is now a private house.

Sir Joseph then set about beautifying the village in 1880, and planted many exotic trees. It was at that time that it became known as Hutton village.

Hutton school was built in 1857 by Sir Joseph Pease for his estate workers' children. The school was well attended, the average attendance in 1890 was 146, and the schoolmaster was a Mr George Henry Angus. The school was converted, after its closure in 1972, into three private residences.

Unfortunately Beeching's axe during the 1960s closed down many branch line stations, and the attractive station at Hutton Gate was one of them. Later the station was converted into a private house; the platform can still be seen, but the signal box has gone. The railway was carried across the road to Hutton village by a stone bridge, part of which still stands, but private houses have been built on the embankment. If the Middlesbrough to Guisborough line via Hutton Gate was still in operation, it would be a very popular and profitable line due to the increase in population of Hutton village and Hutton Gate in recent years.

Ingleby Barwick 🦋

If you ask the present day inhabitants of Ingleby Barwick 'How old is this village?' invariably the answer is, about ten years. Ingleby Barwick is considerably older than ten years. There have been settlements and farms here for over 2,000 years.

In 1970 aerial photographs revealed cropmarks indicating earlier settlements on this site. Excavations revealed the first recognisable residents were men of the Iron Age. The archaeologists discovered that a sizeable percentage of the topsoil was not indigenous to the area. It has been brought upstream and dumped as a result of the extensive building work in Middlesbrough during the 19th century. The cropmarks also show a fairly typical square shape of a Roman fort.

The continuous occupation of this site was not by chance. The Whinstone Dyke, an outcrop of rock at this point of the river, would have created a series of fordable rapids and at the same time be a deterrent to keeled vessels proceeding further upstream. The site may have had strategic military importance. The Normans built a motte and bailey castle at Ingleby Barwick by the junction of the rivers Tees and Leven.

After the Norman Conquest, William gave Ingleby Barwick, along with the parent parish of Stainton, to Robert Malet. Later they were given to Robert de Brus, from whom the Meynalls and the notorious Lucia de Thweng were descended. The younger branch of the de Brus family of Skelton Castle were the antecedents of Robert the Bruce, King of Scotland in 1306. His grandson was the founder of the Stuart line.

When Robert Malet gave the land away it had little or no value. By the time of the Dissolution of the Monasteries it was considered to be of great value. At that time it belonged to Guisborough Priory. From then until the land was sold to Costains property developers in 1969 the land continued to support several farms, and the Great Whinstone Dyke was quarried for the stone, which was in demand for the extensive road building of the 19th century. The rocky projection into the river Tees was also blown up and navigation upstream was made easier.

After the purchase of the land in 1969 the first house was not occupied until 1981. Shops have been built, a health centre and Whinstone primary school. One of the old farmhouses, a listed building, has been extended and modernised and is the village pub, called the Teal inn. *Teal* is the name of a steeplechaser that was trained locally and won the Grand National at Aintree. There is also a church, St Francis. The building comprises two redundant wooden sheds, not great architecture but the heart of the village. In this building all the local activities take place, the play group, St John's Ambulance Brigade, dancing classes and of course the WI. Plans are afoot for a permanent, conventional church building in the future.

Kilton, Kilton Thorpe & Kilton Castle 🌿

After William the Conqueror laid waste to the North, Kilton was worth nothing. The manor was granted to Robert de Brus and then through line of descent to the de Thwengs, who were summoned to sit with the Barons in Parliament in the reigns of Edward I and Edward II. Although other families owned the manorial rights of Kilton, none were so notorious as the de Thwengs.

Pagan Fitzwalter built Kilton Castle sometime in the 12th century, and his family took the name of Kilton. The land belonged to the Percys of Northumberland. The Hauterive family were the next tenants. Matilda de Kilton, widow of Sir Richard Hauterive, was given in marriage, by Lord Percy, to Sir Robert de Thweng. Later historians have dubbed this Robert the 'Robin Hood of Yorkshire'. The Pope was at the time taking every advantage he could to strengthen his power in England. He insisted that Italian priests were given religious livings in England. Robert de Thweng rightly claimed that he would place priests of his own choosing in parishes under his jurisdiction. The Pope placed an Italian in the parish of Kirkleatham and refused to remove him. Robert de Thweng gathered together a band of Norman knights and with this small army robbed every Italian clergyman and his property between the Trent and the Tweed. He stored the loot in Kilton Castle, and then distributed it among the poor.

His great-granddaughter Lucia de Thweng was born in Kilton Castle, and as an heiress of considerable wealth she was made a ward of the King, in the care and protection of her uncle. She was brought up in the company of Marmaduke, her cousin. He was also Lucia's lover. When she was 16 years old Lucia was given in marriage by the King to

William le Latimer, the son of one of his friends. After their marriage William found out that Lucia was pregnant with Marmaduke's baby. She returned to Kilton Castle to live with Marmaduke but their happiness was short lived. At the battle of Stirling in 1297 Marmaduke lost his life. Lucia returned to her husband, and Marmaduke's son was named William le Latimer.

The Scottish war was still raging and William le Latimer was ordered to march north to join the King's army. No sooner had he set off, than Lucia went to live with Peter de Manley at Mulgrave Castle. Then she went and lived with Nicholas de Meynell at Whorlton Castle. Here she had another illegitimate son, Nicholas de Meynell Nothus. Not surprisingly, when William le Latimer returned from the war he divorced Lucia. She then married Sir Robert de Everingham; he too was killed in the Scottish war. Her fourth husband was Sir Bartholomew de Fanacourt.

Lucia died in her manor house at Brotton. During her lifetime she gained the title 'The man eater of Cleveland', usually an appellation given to 20th century filmstars. A shimmering figure in flowing white robes has been seen walking along Kilton Lane. Is this the ghost of Lucia looking for her lost loves? It is not surprising that the history of the de Thwengs overshadows the village of Kilton.

There was a village named Thorpe Chiltun at the time of the Domesday Book and by 1406 it had become Kyleton. This became a deserted village. It only shows up in aerial photography if the light is right, centuries of ploughing have almost obliterated it. There is also a second deserted village, now only a few humps and bumps, a row of miners' cottages, a school which was never used. This is the Victorian village which became obsolete after Kilton mine closed in 1870. Kilton had a population of 86 in 1841. Kilton mill situated at the bottom of Loftus Bank has been restored and modernised and made into a comfortable house.

Kilton Castle is built on a spur of land jutting out into Kilton Ravine. It can only be reached by a field road, and must be one of the most secret castles in England, but well worth a visit. The ruins are private property and permission must be obtained to visit the site. When archaeologists sifted the material that had gathered at the bottom of the well, they discovered the cooked bones of seals, swans, geese, chicken and blackbirds. Was this diet of medieval England?

Kilton today is overshadowed by its larger neighbours of Brotton and Loftus.

Kirkleatham 🦚

The history of Kirkleatham, a very small village near to Redcar, goes back many centuries. Originally called Westlidum, it became Lytham and in the medieval period, Kirkleatham. There were many wealthy owners of the land from the Norman period until John Turner bought the manor in 1623. This was the beginning of a long association of the Turner family with Kirkleatham. John married the daughter of a rich woollen merchant and Kirkleatham was the Turner family home for the next 200 years. St Cuthbert's, the parish church of Kirkleatham, contains a monument to John.

John's second son William was very successful in the woollen business. Eventually he became Lord Mayor of London in 1669. William never forgot his family and the poor of Kirkleatham. He founded and endowed the Sir William Turner Hospital. It was constructed around a rectangular courtyard and open on one side. It accommodated ten poor men and ten poor women on the ground floor, and in the dormitories above ten poor boys and ten poor girls were housed. The adult residents had to be over 63 years of age. The children were issued with uniforms, a long blue coat with brass buttons and a yellow tunic for the boys, while the girls wore blue dresses and yellow petticoats. They were given a basic education at the hospital's small school, and left at the age of 16. They were then presented with a cash reward, and a new suit of clothes to help them at the beginning of their new lives. The last children left the school in the 1930s.

When Sir William died, his great-nephew Cholmley was the main beneficiary of his will. Cholmley had the beautiful chapel built in the almshouses, in memory of Sir William. In this chapel is a magnificent stained glass window, which was designed by Sebastian Ricci, and is reputed to be one of the finest such windows in the world. A death mask of Sir William, made immediately after his death, can be seen on display in the chapel. Kirkleatham Hospital, never a medical establishment, more a place of hospitality, still provides free homes for 20 pensioners.

A clause in Sir William's will stated that he hoped Cholmley would become a woollen merchant – if he didn't, £5,000 must be used to endow a free school at Kirkleatham. He didn't become a woollen merchant and the free school was built. Pupils admitted to the school were all boys, half of whom came from poor families, and the others from wealthy families were expected to subsidise the needy pupils. Over the years 40 pupils from the school were accepted at Cambridge University. Many pupils from the school became doctors, clergymen and lawyers. The school building erected in 1709 is known today as Kirkleatham Old Hall Museum.

Cholmley married Jane Marwood of Busby Hall near Stokesley. When he inherited the Kirkleatham estates he made Kirkleatham Hall his home and pursued a career in politics. He was Member of Parliament for Northallerton, and had to stay for long periods in London. Nevertheless he still spent money, time and effort developing his Kirkleatham estates. The increasing wealth of the Turner family is recorded in the gifts to the poor and a magnificent silver tablepiece commissioned by Cholmley, but now at Temple Newsom, Leeds.

The Reverend Thomas Murgatroyd was appointed master of the free school, and he was also the personal tutor to Marwood, the son of Cholmley. The conflict of loyalty incurred by the two posts was probably the cause of the school having difficulties, and it closed in 1738. Cholmley turned the school into a museum and free library. He donated books and many interesting objects to the collection. The museum attracted many visitors. In his will Cholmley requested that the library and artefacts should be housed at the school for ever, and preserved in memory of his son Marwood. Unfortunately in the 1940s–1950s the entire collection was sold at auction. The only surviving artefact of this collection is the wax death mask of Sir William Turner.

Marwood, Cholmley's son, went on the Grand Tour of Europe after he finished his education at Christ Church Oxford. Tragically he died at Lyon in 1739. His grief stricken family had a monument erected to his memory, a grand mausoleum attached to St Cuthbert's. James Gibb was the architect of this pyramidal mausoleum. The church and the mausoleum are now both Grade I listed buildings.

Jane, Cholmely's widow, was extremely upset when her daughter married Colonel van Strawbenzie, a Dutchman who was here as a foreign mercenary to help suppress the Jacobite rebellion. Jane disinherited her daughter in favour of her brother-in-law William. His son Charles enlarged the Hall, and introduced new farming methods on his land at Hutton Rudby, Crathorne and Ingleby Barwick. The orphan boys from the hospital school were bound as apprentices to Sir Charles' tenant farmers. Uniform farming practices and the modern methods did much to increase efficiency on the estate.

Charles, son of Sir Charles, was the last of the Turners to hold the estates. After his death the old school was used as accommodation for the estate workers. The Charity Commissioners made an enquiry into why it was no longer used as a school, as willed by Sir William. The decision was reached to sell the Old Hall, the money to be used to found the Sir William Turner Grammar School at Coatham. It was opened in 1868. After two further moves it is now Sir William Turner's Sixth Form College on Redcar Lane.

An oddity in Kirkleatham, four railway cottages, built beside old Redcar railway station at Coatham were dismantled white brick by white brick and rebuilt here to house ironstone workers.

In 1956 Kirkleatham Hall was eventually demolished. The site is now Kirkleatham Special School. The Old Hall, the free school, was owned by an Anglo–American family who sold it to Teesside County Council and it is now open to the public as Kirkleatham Old Museum. Perhaps Cholmley rests a little easier now his last wish is partly fulfilled.

Kirklevington & Castle Leavington

The traveller passing on the main Thirsk/Yarm road, the old A19, would note a few bungalows, a public house and 'The Kirk', the country club which to many people in Cleveland, particularly the younger generation, is its only claim to fame. The traveller might be aware of a small church on a knoll and some modern houses. To a stranger Kirklevington could be just a dormitory village to Teesside – but it is worth a much closer look.

Until the county boundary alterations in the early 1970s the village was part of North Yorkshire, but now forms part of the southern boundary of the reorganised County Cleveland and is a community of more than 1,400 people living in just over 300 dwellings.

There is no industry in the village; the majority of the residents work in the neighbouring towns with the remaining minority being employed by the public house, the school, nightclub, shop, car repairer's and agriculture. The working farms and a few cottages are the only survivors of an earlier age, the main part of the village comprising executive-style housing the majority of which was built within the last 25 years.

The Crown Hotel is an old established inn. In earlier times the Crown publican was often the village blacksmith, and the present car repair business is sited near the old forge. The Kirklevington Country Club, a road house with adjoining petrol station, was built in the 1930s.

The 'Old School' dating from 1857 survives and is mainly used by the local playgroup and for small meetings. The school is built on the site of a much earlier property which was the subject of the William Hall Garth Trust. In 1692 William Hall made his will in which he left a property to the people of the village. The proceeds from this were to be distributed to the poor. At a later date the property had fallen into a bad state and the trustees were having difficulty finding needy people, so it was considered that it would be better to replace the derelict buildings with a school, which survives as the 'Old School'.

The new school built in 1973 accommodates in addition to the Kirklevington children, scholars to the age of eleven from neighbouring Picton. The village shop, dating from the start of the modern development, is also a travel agency.

The parish encompasses Kirklevington and Castle Leavington, the latter a scattering of farms with a few modern houses, with the river Leven forming the parish boundary. Alongside the river rises the motte of Castle Leavington, the earliest construction possibly having been erected during the reign of King Stephen (mid 12th century) with a later rebuilding around 1290. It seems unlikely that the castle was inhabited later than the end of the 14th century. The early families of de Brus, Meynell and Percy are associated with the castle.

The church of St Martin at Kirklevington retains its 13th century chancel but earlier stone fragments dating to Saxon times have been found. One of these dated to the 10th century depicting a man's figure with two birds on his shoulders, possibly Odin with his ravens, was displayed in 'The Vikings in England' exhibition in York in 1982.

Two ladies of the parish were instrumental in founding the Bell Fund early in 1989. Sufficient funds were raised to remove, recast and rehang the bells. A few months later the effort was rewarded by a visit from the Bishop of Whitby to lead the service of rededication of the bells of St Martin's.

The vicar at Kirklevington from 1794–1832 was John Graves, who published *The History of Cleveland* in 1808, in which he refers to the early Kirklevington as 'to have been formerly written Leventon (in Domesday Book, Lentune), a name descriptive of its situation; q.d. a town upon the river Leven. The village of Kirklevington was probably so called, as being the town with the parish church; ...'

Two large houses on the outskirts of the village on the Yarm road survive, Kirklevington Grange which is part of the detention centre for young offenders, and Kirklevington

Hall. Both properties were associated with the Richardson family who came from Hartlepool. The Hall was first occupied in 1884 and the estate remained in the family until its sale in 1940. Apart from its time as the centre of the Richardson's estate, the house was used by the Army during the Second World War. Prisoner-of-war pens were constructed, but these were never used. Subsequently the property was the residence of the Justices attending Teesside Crown Court but it has recently been vacated and sold. The legend of the tunnel connecting the two houses is not substantiated.

The village hall, a memorial to the villagers who gave their lives in two World Wars, was opened in 1954, a timber construction paid for by public subscription following many fund raising events from a then much smaller population. Nearby survives the village pump, another reminder of times not so far past.

Thomas Bates, who farmed at Town End Farm, was famous on both sides of the Atlantic as a breeder of short horn cattle. He died in 1849 and is buried in the village churchyard. The farm is still worked and, in addition, has a riding school.

The line of the old Leeds Northern Railway crosses the village and at the time of its construction in the 1840s 'The Hollies', one of the older surviving houses, was used as a cottage hospital for the navvies.

Church House and the adjoining Sun Dial Cottage are of early date, and it is known that one of the latter's occupiers, Elizabeth Passman, had a licence to brew ale.

The village is not unattractive, the older buildings, many heavily restored, blend well with the new housing, as the trees and bushes mature and help soften the more modern lines.

Within the last few years there has been a dramatic change

in industry locally, particularly in steel and petro-chemicals, resulting in far less population movement. This has helped to provide a certain stability of population in Kirklevington and has helped to create a community which resembles more the old-style village life.

Lazenby 🌿

Nestling at the foot of Eston Hills, the ancient village of Lazenby, sandwiched between the ICI south Teesside petro-chemical complex and the castle and grounds of the Wilton estate, is now a dormitory village housing employees of local chemical and steelworks companies.

Entered in the Domesday survey of 1086, Lazenby, a site of Viking origin, enjoyed the rare distinction of being valued by William the Conqueror's agents at the annual rental of one sovereign, this being more than double the value placed on the village during the earlier reign of Edward the Confessor. The higher rate was unusual because most of Cleveland's Saxon manorial holdings had been ravaged by the conquering Normans, lands and habitations being reduced to waste.

For the next 750 years Lazenby remained a rural backwater, its inhabitants working in the fields and grounds of the nearby manor houses and monastic granges. The two-fold impact of the emergence of Teesside's iron mining and steelmaking industries from the 1850s, both events being close to Lazenby, transformed the hamlet from a rural retreat into a rapidly growing village housing a population which had turned its back on agricultural work in order to take up more lucrative employment.

Examination of the census returns shows how rapidly Lazenby discarded its rural traditions. In 1841 there were 57

Lazenby Village

inhabitants, while in 1881 this had risen to 501 inhabitants, a tremendous ten-fold increase within 40 years.

As the village grew so did the servicing requirements so necessary to support the Victorian way of life. By 1867 three nonconformist chapels had appeared and the first local school had been built. Directory entries for 1889 show the growing diversity of the village population with listings including shopkeepers, butchers, blacksmiths, publicans and building trade people. The village's major business centre, Turners Farm, which then specialised in farm machinery, is still in business today.

The 1867 Church of England village school, whose ownership was in 1961 transferred to village trusteeship, had been
a gift from the Lowther family, who as lords of the manor,
were the last to live in the nearby Wilton Castle prior to its
sale to ICI in 1947.

Old village customs were rapidly submerged and lost
during the period of rapid growth. One that did remain was
the annual Glebe House Occasion which occurred on New
Year's Day when village children assembled behind the
Glebe House to recite:

'I wish you a merry Christmas and a Happy New Year
A pocketful of money and a barrel full of beer
Two fat pigs, a new cart and cow
Master and Mistress – how do you do!
Please will you give me a New Year's gift
If you haven't got a penny, a ha'penny will do
If you haven't got a ha'penny, God bless you!'

After singing it together, and properly, the older children
were given an orange, an apple and a penny; each younger
child being given an orange, an apple and a ha'penny.

Old Lazenby had also enjoyed the John Jackson Charity –
a legacy which was set up in 1805 by John Jackson, a planter
in the West Indies, who invested a sum of £500,000, the
annual interest from which was to be given to support the
village poor.

Older inhabitants can remember when people travelled
weekly to Stockton market by horse and cart, and when Mrs
Hard, the local midwife and mortician carried her own
laying-out board around the village when out on 'official'
duty. Mrs Hard also enjoyed the rare distinction of being the
first person in the village to receive the old age pension.

Today Lazenby is a bustling urban village, which, though
dwarfed by the science-fiction panorama of Wilton chemical

works, still retains its own unique separate identity. Rows of ex-miners' cottages lie next to modern developments. The village boasts its own purpose-built primary school and a village shop which stocks the wide range of goods and services essential to modern life. Lying next to the extensive grounds of Wilton Castle and the recreational areas of Eston Hills the village still has much to offer those inhabitants who want to make use of the newly opened leisure facilities of Lazenby Bank and Wilton Woods.

The village people enjoy occasional alarms and confrontations with their huge industrial neighbour, as witnessed by the recent environmental group protest over the proposed Wilton site ENRON/ICI power station with its accompanying forest of electricity supply pylons. Even though they have lost part of this battle the people of Lazenby retain the right to maintain village integrity, a quality which gives the villagers their own sense of pride and belonging. Long may it remain so.

Levendale (Yarm) 🐚

Levendale was, until recent times, an outpost of Yarm. The names of streets on new estates are called after old fields and pathways. The enclosure map of Yarm (1685) shows the names of Slayde, Limpton, The Meadowings and Sheepfoote Hill, thus linking homes to the past.

Old Rose Hill, the house at the corner of Leven Road and Thirsk Road, was the home of the Hedleys, the owners of a nursery garden. The garden land was the old burial ground of St Nicholas' Hospital. The hedge round Old Rose Hill is a double hedge, one side is holly and the other side has a sample of every bush and shrub sold in the original nursery. The Hedleys also owned land where the Kebell estate is, this part of the nursery was used for growing fruit trees. In 1910 its owner claimed that the nursery had been established for 150 years. The entrance to the nursery was opposite to The Grove.

Clock House was originally a farmhouse belonging to the Black Friars, the owners of the Friarage estate. The farm had a dairy attached to it and sold milk locally. Spittal Flatts Farm was the site of one of the new housing estates.

Conyers School along Green Lane is the modern replacement of the old Yarm grammar school founded in 1590. The first grammar school was built in West Street; it is thought that stones from the demolished St Nicholas' Hospital were used.

Today this area serves as a dormitory for Greater Teesside, many people travelling to work in the local chemical and steel industries or in the professions and trades.

Linthorpe 🦢

Deriving from 'Leofa's village', the present name of Linthorpe has also been recorded as Levynthrop, Levingthorp and Linthrop. The original site was near the junction of the present Acklam Road and Burlam Road. The present Linthorpe cemetery was then the village green. 'Levingthorp' also included the hamlets of Ayresome and Newport.

The main farm in the area was Arnold Toft House which is said to have stood on the site of the present-day Little Theatre. This modern building was only erected in the 1950s and opened by Sir John Gielgud in 1957. The company of the Little Theatre itself was formed in 1930 but their productions then took place in St John's church hall on Marton Road.

Linthorpe Road was once known as Linthorpe Lane, being a main route from the original settlement of Middlesbrough. Roman Road was probably an original Roman route as can be seen on the map of Roman Cleveland.

The Blue Hall was a building situated on the corner of Roman Road and Burlam Road. It was reputedly used by smugglers from Newport. Inevitably a rumour exists that there was a subterranean passage from here to the manor house at Acklam, there is, however, no evidence to sustantiate this. The Blue Hall, demolished in 1870, could have been in existence as far back as 1618. Some of the white cottages of Old Linthorpe survived in St Barnabas Road until they were demolished in 1935.

The Victorians were responsible for building the present Linthorpe village which they referred to as New Linthorpe. Albert Park was opened in 1868 by Prince Arthur of Connaught. It has been created in the rural area of Linthorpe and presented by Henry Bolckow, one of Middlesbrough's ironmasters, at a personal cost of £30,000. In 1872 West Lane Hospital was erected on land taken from Linthorpe Cemetery. It was to be a fever hospital.

Also in 1872 the first church services to be held in Linthorpe were in Olive's Gym adjoining the Park Hotel. The following year they were held in the Linthorpe cemetery church. The foundation stones for the first 'proper' church were laid in September 1891. It was in 1897 that this Linthorpe parish church of St Barnabas was opened 'free of debt'.

Linthorpe Schools were originally opened as the Wesleyan day school on 9th January 1871. On that first day the log book reads '14 scholars were admitted'. The first week's fees amounted to three shillings. The number of children gradually increased over the following months. Although absences were common the reasons were investigated and usually logged as being 'satisfactory'. Today the schools are housed in two separate buildings – infant and junior – on the site in Roman Road.

The local Middlesbrough Football Club was formed on 18th February 1876 in the Talbot Hotel. The first recorded game was a draw against Teesside Wanderers in 1877. The matches were then played on the Archery Ground in Albert Park. In 1888 the Football League was formed but the following year the team split into Middlesbrough and Middlesbrough Ironopolis, and introduced professional football. They tried to amalgamate in 1891 but could not agree on a name nor a ground. Ironopolis became financially unsound and folded in 1893. Middlesbrough kepts its amateur status and continued by winning the Northern League. The club moved to Ayresome Park in 1903. Tim Williamson made his debut at Middlesbrough in 1902 and went on to become Boro's first England International player.

Another famous aspect of Linthorpe is found in the history of its pottery which was opened in 1879. It was created out of the old Sun Brick Works which had been owned by Mr John Harrison. The conversion was created under the guidance of Dr Dresser, an architect and designer. The underlying idea was to bring work to idle hands created by the failing iron trade. The local clay was thought to be extremely suitable for the manufacture of high class products.

Linthorpe Pottery was noted for the boldness of colour and high glaze. It became known worldwide at the London International Exhibition of 1885. It was here that Princess Alexandra of Wales purchased an example. The pottery secured a medal, and more prizes were won at New Orleans and Calcutta. Orders began to pour in from all over the world. However, this success was short-lived as Mr Harrison ran into financial troubles after the failure of another of his companies. So production at the Linthorpe Pottery ceased in

1889. It was sold by auction in 1891. Many examples can still be seen in the local Dorman Museum.

In 1897 the site of the pottery was proposed as a zoological garden – Belle Vue Gardens. This promised a dance room, side shows, sensations and novelties, fireworks and a permanent zoological collection with hundreds of strange animals and birds – all for sixpence! Some 20,000 people attended the opening but found it to be some sort of hoax. There were hardly any attractions, just a few meagre cages of monkeys and birds were on show. It lasted seven days and, apparently, for weeks afterwards the bodies of the animals were seen floating on the Pottery Pond. Belle Vue Road is said to be named after the ill-fated zoo and is the only reminder of this fanciful project. More recently the site of the pottery was used as a laundry.

One of the more recent buildings in the area is the Carter Bequest Hospital. It was originally intended for the benefit of less fortunate people. It has since been used as a private hospital and is now a local hospice.

Today people of the area refer to Linthorpe as 'The Village' although it is mainly the shopping area at the southern end of Linthorpe Road to which they refer. The community of Linthorpe extends between the areas of Ayresome, Acklam, Tollesby and Middlesbrough town itself. It is very much alive and varied in its population. There is even a fairly new community centre situated in 'The Village' which holds popular classes and events on a regular basis, distributing newsletters to the local community.

Liverton 🦜

Liverton is a small village of no more than 20 houses, a few farms, a new bungalow and a relatively new house, now privately owned, that was once the police house when Liverton was in the North Riding of Yorkshire.

Liverton is mentioned in the Domesday Book, when its name was Liureton. Until recently the farms were mostly owned by Lord Downe of Scarborough, and the iron ore mine at Liverton was also owned by his family. The first mine was sunk in 1866, but Liverton escaped being developed as a dormitory for the influx of miners to the area from all over the country. Liverton has retained its rural farming community atmosphere even to the present day. Now it is protected by a conservation order.

The church of St Michael was built in the 12th century, remodelled in the 18th century, and further improved in 1902. St Michael's was a chapel of ease for Easington and was granted to Guisborough Priory in 1218. The church has a magnificent Norman chancel arch, with carved capitals, one of which depicts a wild boar hunt. The font bowl and a grave slab bear the Fitz–Conan arms. There is also a Jacobean chest, table and two medieval bells.

Thomas Parrot, a Quaker of Liverton was fined and deprived of goods to the value of £28-4 shillings, because he had not paid his tithes. There was a Quaker burial ground to the north-west of the village. A mill was situated near to Kilton beck.

The village, because of its preservation order, cannot be enlarged, improved or altered. The old village school, originally donated by Lord Downe is now the village hall. Liverton has its own hostelry, the Water Wheel inn. Liverton village is a secluded haven protected from the hurly-burly of the 20th century.

Loftus 🌿

Loftus, or Lofthouse, as it was previously spelled before the advent of the railways, derives its name from the Scandinavian word 'lopthus' meaning a house with a loft or upper storey. As can be imagined this would have been quite a landmark in an area where most buildings would be single storey.

Loftus has developed from an ancient settlement in a valley between the moors and the sea. Remains of a prehistoric settlement have been excavated within the area and Loftus is mentioned in the Domesday Book. The alum mines of the 17th century were probably responsible for Loftus's early development towards a township and the ironstone mines brought about a doubling of the population in the 1860s. Both of these industries are now defunct. Strangely a tunnel emerged from the cliff face between Hummersea and Boulby, which led into part of the workings of Loftus mine, and there the miners were able to wave to the fishermen, fishing off Boulby, during their meal breaks.

Loftus has been a market town for many years and has always provided a focal point for the outlying areas. The ancient Wool Fair continued until fairly recently, the final one being in 1938, with the advent of the Wool Board. Recently a committee was formed to revive the Wool Fair and in 1989 a very successful attempt was made to do so, although the inherent 'wool' of the Wool Fair was replaced by a feeling of celebration of an old market rather than the selling of the fleeces as in the old days. There is a building situated between the present post office and the town hall which was previously the wool warehouse.

Since 1989 a Dickensian week has been held in the town in early December when the locals are encouraged to dress up in Dickensian-style costume as they go about their daily

The Market Place at Loftus

business. Dances, street theatre and a market are also part of the week's entertainment.

The old village of Loftus is the area around the market place where buildings of local sandstone predominate. North Road was the main area of business closely followed by Dam Street or Dam Side as it was originally called. Dam Street housed the Black Bull pub, a chapel, the workhouse and the police station as well as several commercial concerns and many cottages now sadly lost. It is interesting to note that Gaskille Lane was once the main thoroughfare through Loftus, now very much a backwater.

The parish church of St Leonard was built by Ignatius Bonomi in 1811 but the west tower is the only substantial part of his church to survive, today's church having been rebuilt between 1888–1901. There have been many chapels in Loftus, the present parish hall used to be the Congregational chapel, which now stands at the crossroads at Station Road, a fine building with a unique outdoor pulpit used for open air services. The Newton Memorial chapel used to stand on Chapel Bank near East Crescent, an imposing building which was bombed during the Second World War. The Arlington Street Methodist chapel was built in 1870 and the Arlington Hotel stood between the two chapels. For this reason the hotel was denied a Sunday licence, which was only granted after the Newton Memorial chapel was destroyed in the war. The first Primitive Methodist chapel was one of the buildings on Dam Street now lost.

In the late 1800s early 1900s the areas of Zetland Road and West Road developed, along with that of Coronation Road in the 1930s. A large council estate was built in the 1970s adding little to the character of the town; on the other hand a new housing estate just off the North Road car park has been built and planned to very high standards and is most aesthetically pleasing.

The site on which the supermarket stands in the Market Place was where the manor house once stood, possibly the home of Zachary Moore, lord of the manor, in the 18th century. The Angel inn was formerly a coaching inn and Pear Tree Cottage, also in the Market Place, is reputedly the oldest brick-built house in the town. Prospect Cottage on Micklow Lane is said to be the oldest stone cottage in Loftus.

Loftus Hall was built in 1840 for Robert Dundas, who was lord of the manor at that time. The hall is an imposing building now divided up to make several homes. The stable block of the Hall is now home to the YTS scheme and Stable House is used by a local women's group. The Lodge to the Hall grounds was built in 1863 and is now a private house.

Cromwell House is also a well known landmark in Loftus.

Cromwell is reputed to have slept there, but as the house was not built until the 18th century this would seem to be impossible! Another interesting house also situated near East Crescent is Old Beck Cottage, a two storey cottage the ground floor of which is said to date from about 1700. The Station Hotel is another of Loftus's fine old buildings, the local magistrate's court was held there before the town hall was built and the locals played quoits in the yard. There was also a photographer's studio to the rear of the Station Hotel.

The local paper was *The Loftus Advertiser*, which was printed behind the shop, which is still a newsagent's, at Station Road. It is gratifying that in recent years a new paper has been born called *The Loftus Town Crier*. This small magazine covers local events and popular comment but also prints recollections of local people's memories of Loftus as it was. It is printed by Loftus Employment Training who now occupy the old Co-op buildings in the High Street and who provide jobs and training for the people of the town. The Co-op was originally built by local ironstone miners, as was the Odd Fellows Hall which was one of the eleven friendly societies in the town, providing sickness, injury and widow's benefits to its members who saved with the society each week.

The railway reached Loftus in 1867 when the spelling of Lofthouse was changed to avoid confusion with another Lofthouse in the West Riding. Loftus is still quite a lively community and retains its rural air. Most people find their employment at Boulby Potash Mine, Skinningrove Iron and Steel Works or on Teesside.

Longnewton 🦢

'Long New Town', as the name suggests, is a moderate-sized village about four miles west of the township of Stockton. Few people realise that the village of Longnewton was the setting for an act of great significance for one of our country's oldest universities. Somewhere around 1255 a row between John Balliol and Walter de Kirkham, Bishop of Durham, led John Balliol, the lord of the manor, and his friends to seek sanctuary in Longnewton church. The Bishop excommunicated the offenders, but after six weeks they were still unmoved and the Bishop had them arrested. Balliol's friends later attacked the Bishop and took four of the Bishop's men prisoners. The King ordered Balliol to release the men and make retribution to the Bishop for their sins against the Church.

John Balliol's punishment was severe. Even though he was a great noble, he was ordered to receive a personal reprimand from the Bishop himself at the door of Durham Cathedral. It was also a requirement of his retribution that he settle a sum of money to keep a fixed number of students at the University of Oxford. The founding of the scholarship took place in about 1263. After John Balliol's death, his wife founded Balliol college in his memory.

The first of the Vane family who came to Longnewton was George, brother of Sir Harry Vane of Raby Castle, who was beheaded in 1662 at the time of King Charles II. His great-grandson, Rev Henry Vane, was rector of Longnewton, and in 1768 he married a rich heiress, Frances Tempest of Wynyard. His son, another Sir Henry, left Longnewton and went to live in the manor house at Wynyard. The Vane mansion was let in apartments for a while before being eventually pulled down, leaving only the orchard, walls, and the gateposts. Today only the walls and the gateposts

St Mary's Church, Longnewton

remain. After Sir Henry's death in 1813, the estates were left to his only child – Frances Anne Vane Tempest. She married the third Marquis of Londonderry who took the name of Vane-Tempest-Stewart.

There has been a church at Longnewton for over 800 years, but the present church of St Mary was constructed in 1856, under the direction of the Marchioness of Londonderry. Two years previously Lady Frances has decided to erect a mausoleum over the old family vault in the church crypt. Many plaques still exist in the church today, including one to George Vane who died in 1679 and his wife Elizabeth who died in 1684. The mausoleum was built in a 13th century style but was positioned behind a double screen of pointed arches on the north side of the chancel, more or less out of sight.

The church itself was designed in 14th century style, and the nave and chancel had the same dimensions as the 1806 building. An effigy of the third Marquis of Londonderry carved in marble by Monti was placed in the centre of the mausoleum chamber. The effigy was removed in 1904 to the monument room at Wynyard Hall. By way of compensation the Marquis paid for a chancel screen to match the new choir stalls and pulpit. The present Lord Londonderry's parents are interred in the Londonderry chapel.

There are no records of any major repairs having been carried out since 1857, and so that St Mary's church, a focal point in Longnewton, can continue to serve an ever increasing community, a major restoration scheme is now being planned. The first recorded rector was Peter de Brandon in 1259 and the parish register dates from 1564.

Other buildings of interest in the village are the community centre, which used to be the old school, and an old Methodist chapel, sadly no longer used for worship.

There is also the Wilson Institute which dates from 1887. It is a good brick building and its original purpose was as a free library and reading room; it is still in constant use today, and this is the building where the Women's Institute hold their monthly meetings. It is also used for public entertainment and will seat 150. There is a new primary and junior school in the village now, this was opened in March 1973 and the new St Mary's school makes its own unique contribution to the life of the village.

Longnewton has one village shop turned post office which has been in the village for about 40 years.

The village still keeps its village identity with a yearly show which is held the second week in September. There used to be floats which were made by the villagers and these were paraded from the west end of the village to the east end, but these have now given way to the more traditional fancy dress parade.

Also of great interest in the village are the resident rare Natterer's Bats. Of around 60 roost sites in Cleveland and North Yorkshire, this is the only one where Natterers are found. They can be seen from May to September. Each night at dusk they emerge from their roosts to fly and feed. Also in the pipeline at the moment is a plan to turn some spare woodland at the west end of the village into a nature reserve.

The main road winds quietly through the village now, although it was originally the main road between Stockton and Darlington. The A66 now bypasses the village. There are still farms within the village boundaries but the housing has been extended by new building. A visitor may notice that Longnewton is a green village – both ends of the village show long front gardens which indicates that there were two village greens in days of old. There are still two village greens but now differently sited.

When the housing estate at the west end of the village was built a new resident could not dig his garden because he struck brick. The builders still on site discovered a tunnel stretching across the green, brick-lined and with fresh air. One workman ventured into the tunnel, but his courage failed after 100 yards and he came back and the entrance was closed.

In the village there are two public houses, the Londonderry Arms and the Vane Arms (the latter used to be called the New Inn). Their names reflect the village's history.

Maltby 🌿

In J. W. Ord's book *The History and Antiquities of Cleveland*, Maltby is described as 'an indifferently built village, perched on an eminence three and a half miles east by north of Yarm.'

Maltby was in existence long before this was written in 1846. It was a Danish settlement. In 1086 it was called Maltebi, derived from the Danish meaning 'Malti's Farm'. At the time of the Domesday Book it is recorded that Maltby consisted of three carucates of land, one carucate being about 160 acres. Maltby was under the jurisdiction of the manor of Acklam. By 1810 Sir James Pennyman held all the principal land, while the remaining land was held by the Earl of Harewood and John Goldsborough, which they sold at a later date.

Maltby is in the parish of Stainton and during the Reformation the Catholic villagers carried their dead in the middle of the night to Stainton churchyard and buried them there according to the Roman Catholic rites. They refused to adopt the new Protestant religion. In the past Maltby beck abounded in fish and eels. These fisheries belonged to the religious houses at Guisborough and Byland.

Maltby has its own coat of arms: a silver shield bearing a red diagonal with gold sheaves of corn.

As you approach Maltby there is a ridge of land which harbours many interesting plants and shrubs. It is reputed to be Tudor in origin and possibly the site of a lost church. The villagers tend the plants with care. The field behind is an ancient burial ground.

Maltby is a street village built in the days of horse power, consequently in the day of the car there are continuous parking problems. There are several interesting houses in the village, fine examples of various building styles, and some are listed. One house, a tall thin structure, is reputed to have a donkey buried in the back garden! The village at one time had a cooper, a wheelwright, a potter and a seed and grain merchant.

Maltby House belonged to the Watson family. Their daughter, Miss Lucy, ran the Sunday school in the house. There wasn't a doctor in the village, and if a person needed to go to Middlesbrough Hospital they had to request 'a ticket' from the Watson family. This ticket was confirmation that the person needed qualified medical attention. Maltby House was situated at the western end of the village.

One of the farmhouses is built from hand-made Dutch bricks. They were brought from Holland as ballast in the ships coming up to Yarm. The outgoing ships were laden with wool. This farmhouse has some wonderful carved sailing ships on the barn doors. Did some farm lad dream of the sea while working on the land?

Maltby today is still a street but has sprouted two developments of bungalows at each end of the village. A further development has taken place of eleven houses and bungalows at the west end of the village, called Pennyman Green.

The village shop is the meeting place where people exchange news and read the notices of forthcoming events. We would fare very badly without this excellent little shop. The local hostelry, the Pathfinders, is the venue for many village events.

The small Methodist chapel is kept alive by eight stalwart members. The chapel was built over a hundred years ago, with bricks made mainly at Bousefield brickworks at Grange Farm. They were carted to Maltby free of charge by local farmers. The chapel is open for Sunday evening service at 6.30 pm, a Christmas carol service and an annual strawberry tea.

Villagers have managed to get an ancient footpath reopened. Originally a farmworkers' 'trod', it was a short cut between Maltby and Hilton. Negotiations are underway to reopen another footpath, a circular route, Maltby–Thornton–Maltby.

The village hall is an ex-army hut from the Second World War. A wooden edifice, put up in 1952, it is lovingly cared for and tucked away off the main street.

Some residents can trace their ancestry back three centuries just by looking at the parish records of Stainton church. Maltby may be small, but as the Britain in Bloom judges said 'It is a very pleasant village in which to live.'

Margrove Park 🦢

Margrove Park, commonly referred to as 'Maggra Park' or 'Maggra', takes its name from a nearby farm and from the deer park that was in the vicinity in years gone by. A hunt called the Warren Hunt operated in the area from Skelton Castle until the mid 1950s.

The houses were built in a square in the 1850s to house miners. Stanghow (Margrove Park) mine still has a tall air shaft making it a landmark. Thomas Ward dismantled the mine in 1930. A bystander at the time remembers that they couldn't make the mine shaft fall so they loaded a truck of stone on a train, fastened it to the shaft and with a steady pull it fell. Sleepers were sold from there for sixpence, some still evident in gardens. The row of shops which formed the bottom of the square – grocer's, cobbler's and shoeshop, fish shop and a big dancing pavilion, were pulled down because of lack of use or mining subsidence in the 1930s. There are no shops in the village now. The village used to be served by the Charltonian bus but there is now a half hourly service from Guisborough.

In 1940 the houses were sold to the occupiers for £160, a mortgage being available from Guisborough Provident Society (Co-operative). It was paid back at ten shillings per week with the grocery bill.

In 1932 when the mines closed and unemployment was rife, Major James Beaumont Pennyman had the idea of making allotments on Heartbreak Hill just outside Margrove Park. It was a rocky place. The men started to work and were helped by university students who slept in the old mine offices. Any vegetable produce grown was sold and then seeds bought to be put back into the land. The men earned a halfpenny an hour but no money was given, wages were in kind. It cost one shilling and threepence to mend ladies shoes so a man worked 30 hours in order to have them repaired. A man's shoes cost one shilling and ninepence.

Prince George came to visit the Heartbreak Hill project in the 1930s, at the same time planting a tree at Guisborough grammar school and giving the boys a half day's holiday. The scheme went on for some years.

Opposite the bottom side of the square of Margrove Park is the bird-watching area of the Carrs, with Canada Geese and many other migrating birds. The area around 'Maggra' is most attractive, with trees, fields, bushes and hills and rusty soil which reveals the iron ore which used to abound. There were two large shale heaps in the area but they have been removed and used for the foundations of buildings in the Guisborough area.

A large caravan site houses the many holidaymakers who come to the beautiful nearby coastal area, increasingly many German and Dutch visitors. The old school on the main road has been made into a Heritage Centre. Here one can see models of Iron Age man with his artefacts and the abundant flora and fauna of the area. There is also a good space for the display of exhibitions and crafts.

Marske by the Sea ✑

Very few people outside of the county of Cleveland have heard of Marske. Long ago its more famous sisters of Saltburn, Redcar and Coatham were only part of the parish of Marske. Before the Conquest, Earl Tostig gave land at Mersc (Marske) for a church. This church was built on the headland and dedicated to St Germaine. There were only seven priests in the whole of Cleveland and one was appointed to Marske. Mersc is the Old English for marsh. When the Normans were laying waste to the North, Marske was left untouched and in fact had increased in value.

St Germaine's church has been rebuilt several times on the same foundations. When the church of St Mark was built in 1867 the church authorities decided to demolish St Germaine's. There are two stories about this demolition. The first, and most probably the mundane true story, is that the walls were so solidly built they had be blown up with gunpowder. Legend tells a different tale. Every day the demolition gang set about knocking the walls down. Every night a gang of 'Hob Men' (unearthly creatures) built them up again. Eventually the authorities won by default, so the locals said, and they blew them up with gunpowder. The tower still stands. The site of the old church is said to be haunted by the ghost of Will Watch, whose real name was William Stainton. He was a notorious smuggler and church official who stored his ill gotten gains within the church. Perhaps the ghost of Will Watch was the leader of the Hob Men?

The church of St Mark has a large, Norman square font, originally at St Germaine's. For more than 80 years it lay neglected, then was taken to a farmyard, from where it was rescued by one of the vicars of Marske and taken to his garden where he had it planted with flowers. Rescued once again it was placed in St Mark's along with a Saxon cross which had been found in the sand dunes in 1901. Captain Cook's father is buried just a short distance from the old tower of St Germaine's.

There is a lady living in Marske renowned for her memory; she is Charlotte Hughes, a former schoolteacher, and the oldest living person in England. In 1990 she celebrated her 114th birthday. When she went to America on Concorde she astounded the world with her mental alertness at her great age.

The most famous building in Marske is Marske Hall, built in 1625 by Sir William Pennyman. A Royalist, he was forced to sell it at a fraction of its value to pay the fines imposed on him by Cromwell's government. A later tenant of the Hall was William Penn the famous Quaker, founder of Pennsylvania. Today Marske Hall is a Cheshire Home for the physically handicapped. The Earl of Zetland made a gift of the Hall to this worthy charity.

Another fine house in Marske is Cliff House, built by Joseph Pease in 1844. In 1930 it was sold to the Holiday Fellowship of the Methodist Church. They moved out in 1974, and after a period of vandalism and weather erosion it was purchased by the Church Army and made into retirement homes.

Marske was affected by the iron ore boom. The demand for houses was partly resolved by Messrs Pease building 3,000 cottages in Marske followed by the development at New Markse.

The long flat beach at Marske was the venue for the flight by Robert Blackburn in 1909. It attracted a large crowd of awe-struck spectators. Malcolm Campbell used this beach when practising for his attempt on the land speed world record. The severe storms of 1953 devastated the beach and washed away a lot of sand, revealing rocks that had never been seen before.

The Anderson Brothers, shoe repairers of Marske, bought 162 High Street, the oldest cottage, about 400 years old. They set about restoring it, and have made it into an interesting folklore museum, known as 'Winkies Castle'.

The population of Marske is more than 15,000 and still growing. There are many new houses and a fairly young population, who are employed in the various industrial complexes in the Tees valley.

The local cricket club is a thriving concern, again thanks to the generosity of the Lord of Zetland who donated the land. The present Ship inn is the last of a long line of hostelries of that name that have all been on this site. Marske is the home of the renowned Apollo male voice choir. With the Yorkshire National Park to the landward, and the sandy beach stretching from Saltburn to South Gare on the seaward, Marske is a thriving, pleasant place to live.

Marton & Tollesby

Soon after the Norman Conquest, the present parish of Marton, like much of North Yorkshire, was in the overlordship of the powerful de Brus family. They founded Guisborough Priory about 1120 and they were donors of land to this priory as well as to the abbeys of Whitby and Byland.

About this period the present church of Marton was built and dedicated to St Cuthbert. No record of it being built is known to exist but it was given to Guisborough Priory, together with pieces of land in the manors of Marton and Tollesby, possibly before 1187. When Henry VIII brought about the Dissolution of the Monasteries in 1545, the living of Marton was granted to the See of York, to which it has

Captain Cook Museum, Marton

ever since belonged. Until the late 18th century the only big house in the parish was at Tollesby. This was probably the home of the Foster family, who were lords of this manor from early in the 17th century. It was in a state of decay at the beginning of the 19th century.

Marton's most distinguished son, Captain James Cook RNFRS, was born on 27 October 1728 in a simple thatched cottage and baptised at Marton church on 3rd November.

In 1786 Bartholomew Rudd bought the manor of Marton from Sir John Ramsden. Work started on a house, Marton Lodge, which stood where the conservatory now stands. It was surrounded by a landscaped park, which covered approximately the western two-thirds of present Stewart Park.

A national census carried out in 1801 showed Marton to contain 342 people living in 80 houses. Of these 180 were employed in agriculture. Graves in the *History of Cleveland* (1808) said 'the soils near the village are fertile. Rich old pastures and tilled land'.

In 1843–46 the original St Cuthbert's church, which had been built in the 12th century, was restored. Plans were drawn up in the early 1840s for the first stage of the restoration under the direction of J. B. Rudd Esq of Tollesby. The aim of the plan appears to have been to restore the church to its original dimensions.

At the instigation of Bartholomew Rudd a fund was raised to build a village school in memory of James Cook. The land was given by Rev J. A. Park, who also allowed all the stone needed to be taken from the ruins of Marton Lodge. The school closed in 1961, when a new school opened.

A railway line was opened just inside the eastern boundary of the parish in 1850. This was part of the Middlesbrough to Guisborough railway company, principally to bring ore from the mines at Hutton Lowcross to the furnaces of Messrs Pease and Partners in Middlesbrough. The first ore train ran in November 1850 and the first passenger train in February 1854.

Albert Park, which had been given to the town by Henry Bolckow, was opened by Prince Edward, son of Queen Victoria and later Duke of Connaught. Following this, on the evening of 11th August 1868, Henry Bolckow gave a ball at Marton Hall in honour of the prince, who was staying there as his guest. Two marquees were erected in the grounds, one for dancing and one for supper.

In 1968 Marton Parish Council ceased to exist, becoming part of Middlesbrough. Just before this happened, a stone from the headland of Point Hicks (which was the first land in Australia sighted by Captain Cook) was erected on the village green, and dedicated by the Hon Sir Horace Petty, Agent General of Victoria, Australia. In 1978 the Captain Cook Birthplace Museum was built in Stewart Park. It stands some 200 yards from the site of the cottage where James Cook was born in 1728. The cottage was demolished when the grounds of Marton Lodge were laid out in 1858. Henry Bolckow erected a granite vase on the site. Members of Marton Women's Institute made clothes for the model of the young James Cook in the museum.

In September 1989 a fund was opened to raise £300,000 for a new parish centre. The main hall is to be named the James Cook Hall. A memorial to Captain Cook, which had been removed from the church at its restoration in 1843 and built into the wall of the main classroom of the Captain Cook Memorial school, was returned to the church and it was unveiled on 5th November 1989.

Moorsholm 🌿

Moorsholm means a collection of houses or huts surrounded by heath. Ord (1846) described Moorsholm as a 'dismal prototype of Goldsmith's Deserted Village, undecorated by any appliances of modern civilisation or recent improvement', but the old delapidated thatched cottages have given place to well-built houses with all the modern conveniences. The present population of Moorsholm, around 400 people, is a mixture of local farming families, commuters, who work mainly in the Teesside conurbation, and retired people. Thankfully Goldsmith's epithet is no longer applicable.

Freebrough Hill is a conspicuous landmark on the Guisborough to Whitby (A171) road, a mile south of Moorsholm. This strange symmetrical hill has been the subject of much debate by historians and laymen alike. Many assume it to be man-made and some kind of burial ground. This and other speculation is chronicled by Ord (1846) and Bulmer (1890). However, geologists have shown that Freebrough Hill is entirely natural, its stratas of rock and boulder clay are the same as the surrounding countryside.

109

Spout House, High Street, Moorsholm is a long sandstone building which stands back from the west side of the village street, north of the church and church hall. It is a longhouse and in its simplest form was a single-storey building with the living part at one side and a byre at the other separated by a cross passage, which had front and back doors. Above the doorway is an initialled shield and the date 1695. A detailed survey (1985) lists the rebuilding and subsequent alterations. In the summer of 1985 the then present population of the village gathered on the lawn of Spout House to pose for a photograph which was included in the modern-day Domesday Project, Moorsholm also being mentioned in the original Domesday Book.

At no time did the village have a live railway but it did have a railway hotel. 'Paddy Waddell's Railway' or 'The Cleveland Extension Mineral Railway' was the railway that was never finished. When the railway was proposed in 1872 Miss E. Marsay's grandfather built the Station Hotel at a cost of £1,600 on a well-chosen corner site adjacent to the present village hall. But the anticipated trade from the nearby railway never materialised. For a few years an off-licence business was conducted until the house became the private home of the family, known locally as 'the big house' or 'Hillock's House'. Sadly, it was demolished in 1989. Other relics of the proposed railway are strange incomplete earthworks, remnants of embankments and cuttings, cast-iron and brick-built culverts which can be found in the fields around Moorsholm. There were plans for houses and shops on Charlton's Fields which were never built.

Jimmy Johnson, born in 1911, and other residents in the village have memories and recollections which are of great value in building up a picture of the social history in the locality. He remembers Mr Jekyll, nicknamed 'Billy Blobs', the headmaster of the village school. He was once invited to the headmaster's house for tea and to listen to the wireless, a rare treat in those days. The school built in 1876, with the main entrance overlooking open fields, was to have been part of the new main village street but the development never took place. The school was closed in 1968, although this was strongly opposed by local people. It is now Manor Court residential home for the elderly. At Christmas Jimmy remembers getting up early in the morning and walking to Gerrick 'calling' at the farms in the hope of being given coppers or, best of all, a 'silver threepenny piece'.

Jimmy left school at 14. His final job was working for NRCC. His workmate at the time, Isaac Theaker, asked him, 'What kind of cargo comes in at "Moorsholm Docks"?' Jimmy was able to explain that it was the name some local wag had given to six drinking troughs for horses and cattle in the High Street. Old threshing machines and steam rollers were also filled with water from the docks, the old course of which started behind Freebrough Hill and can be traced around the village. The pinfold where stray beasts were rounded up and put until their owners had paid a 'fine' to get them out is situated between Manor Farm and 31 High Street opposite the church hall.

The village hall, officially opened in 1957 as a memorial to those men from the village who died in the two world wars, is used for many village activities. A weekly doctor's surgery is also held there.

The village pub, now called the Toad Hall Arms, but formerly the 'Plough Hotel', has the usual activities of darts, dominoes, quoits and quizzes. Every year they have a Harvest Festival auction and the money goes to the senior citizens at Christmas.

The Jolly Sailors inn, Moorsholm, is situated just off the A171 Whitby to Guisborough road, the original road having once passed the door of the building. The inn dates back to

1755, Captain Cook's era, when Whitby was a flourishing sea port. Legend has it that the crews left the ships and made their way across the moors with two or three years pay in their pockets. If they weren't robbed by highwaymen, they stopped at the inn and spent their wages on food and drink – hence the name.

New Markse 🌿

In 1849 the area now known as New Marske consisted of six farms. Five of these are still worked today, the other one is a livery stable. In 1849 these all belonged to the Dundas family. In 1851 the Derwent Iron Company negotiated with Lord Zetland (the head of the Dundas family) to mine some acres of land at the foot of the Upleatham hills. Eventually work began at the top end of what is now known as the village of New Marske.

The mining company was eventually bought out by Joseph Pease and drifts were opened on the east end of Errington Woods. Pease and Partners built houses to accommodate the workers and the village was formed. These houses were well constructed and are still occupied today. They have been modernised and are worthwhile properties now.

The Quaker employers enforced a ban on profane and improper language. No public house was provided. Today there are three! In 1865 a pub was built between Marske and New Marske, but this was never granted a licence, and therefore was never opened. Today this building has been renovated and made into two delightful cottages.

In 1874 Pease and Partners built a village school, a church hall, an institute, and a Wesleyan chapel. The land was given by Lord Zetland. He also paid for the building of St Thomas's church in 1875.

When the railway was extended to Saltburn a branch line was built up to the village, and ended just below the mine entrance. When the mine was closed the railway line was demolished.

Allotments were provided and the miners were able to grow their own vegetables, rear poultry and pigs in an effort to feed their families. True to tradition the miners formed their own silver band, which led many demonstrations, played for the Psalm Sunday procession, the Christmas carol service and the Remembrance Day parade and many other events. In 1958 after many years of faithful service in New Marske the band moved to Marske. The Band Hall in the village was taken down to make way for further developments.

A local builder built new houses from the top of Chapel Bank upwards to Errington Woods. This was the beginning of the extension to New Marske and was called Errington Park. This brought new life to the old village. Shops were built, and Government grants were used to modernise the old properties. Thanks to the hard work and enterprise of the Reverend Alan Hughes the old church hall was taken down, and in 1981 a new hall was built. Also in 1981 New Marske was granted parish status and in September of that year Rev Hughes was installed as the first vicar of New Marske. The old Wesleyan chapel was badly damaged by fire and a new one was erected.

Two new schools have been built to replace the old one, which has been extensively renovated by the council and is now run by members of the village as a community centre. New Markse is a lively, healthy village with the sea to the east and Errington Woods to the west.

Newsham

Newsham (Anglo-Saxon meaning 'the new dwelling') takes its place name from a settlement around about the 12th century, evidence of which can be seen today along the top of the river Tees bank overlooking the village of Worsall in North Yorkshire. Lines of walls, house foundations and other earthworks can still be traced, also the chapel of St James which was sequestered by the Bishop Langley in 1414 for non-payment of rent. This village ceased to exist by 1600.

In the early 1800s, Newsham comprised an area of approximately 1,000 acres, divided into four farms, Featherstone House, Newsham Hall, Newsham Grange and White House. Newsham Hall estate has been reduced over the years as houses and parcels of land were sold off. The area now

The Hall, Newsham Village

consists of Newsham Hall, Newsham House, Newsham Grange, Thornhill, Rose Cote, Featherstone House and Grey House. Church services have been held in a summerhouse attached to Newsham Hall since 1871. This summerhouse could have been a forerunner of the Hall we have today, as no records can be traced as to when the present Hall was built.

In the late 1800s and early 1900s local people could come to the mission hall, as it was then called, and borrow library books for one penny per month, an old record book can be seen in the Hall to this day. A Sunday school was also held in the hall from the early 1920s to the early 1930s on a Sunday afternoon, the Rev A. T. Dingle from Egglescliffe parish church travelling by bicycle to take part. Each child was given a white mint to suck while he told stories from the Bible. The Watts family from Newsham House always attended this Sunday school. Church services were held once a month. Social activities during this period consisted of the local farmers and workers playing cricket on a Sunday in a field adjoining Newsham Hall. The Church Army used to come to the Hall from time to time and show slides, and different farmers' wives would put on an evening meal for them every time they came. Fishermen used to come from the Stockton area on Saturdays and Sundays, having taken some form of transport to Butts Lane, then walking the rest of the way to the river at Newsham.

Children were transported to Egglescliffe Church of England school in Butts Lane by a horse and carriage in the early 1920s, this belonging to a family called Raper who were the local undertakers. As more children came into the area a horse and four-wheeled wagon together with a tarpaulin cover, came into use, the boys having to get out and push to help the wagon up Aislaby bank. Eventually the era of the bus came and made things a lot easier. Housewives were also allowed to use this bus on Stockton market day for the purpose of shopping.

One notable character of the area was Mr Charlie Bunn who had a small market garden at Thornhill. He used to take his vegetables by horse and cart to Stockton every Saturday and was well known around various streets there as he sold his produce. When his horse needed shoeing Mr Bunn would take it across the ford in the river, the horse was shod and returned via the river.

Present day people are still mostly in agriculture, though a few travel out of the village to work in offices. Children still go to Egglescliffe schools, now travelling by taxi as numbers are once again very few. Parties of school children and members of various societies often come to have a look at the site of the ancient village. No more do we have travelling shops, newspapers delivered, bread vans calling; now just the postman and coalman and more cars and heavy motor vehicles than these old roads were ever meant to take.

Newton under Roseberry 🌿

Roseberry Topping is, due to erosion, just short of 1,000 ft high and is the landmark of Cleveland. The actual peak is in North Yorkshire but the county line is about a third of the way up the hill. Sitting at the base is the hamlet of Newton under Roseberry.

The graveyard has been in use since Saxon times. By the south wall is a huge stone coffin, over seven ft long. It was discovered in 1827. There are several ancient stones inset into the wall of the church. This church, dedicated to St Oswald, is 12th century but the font is decorated with Norman carvings. It became a parish church at the Dissolution of the Monasteries. Opposite the lychgate is the manor house built in the late 17th century.

There was a holy well on the side of Roseberry Topping. It was reputed that if you drank the water it would cure many of the then prevalent illnesses. Quarrymen unfortunately demolished the well and the water was piped some distance away.

Newton's Trinity Mass Fair was held for many years and was famous throughout the district. Early in the morning of the fair the vicar, churchwardens, choir, and of course those of the congregation that could manage it, climbed to the top of Roseberry Topping, where the Trinity Mass was held. On this day, this quiet village became the hub of entertainment. Jugglers, actors, stalls and funfairs were all there. Outsiders would arrive before first light to make the most of the day. When the Reverend E. Tugman became the vicar of Newton he abolished this fair because it was held on God's day, the Sabbath.

Today Newton under Roseberry, an unspoilt village, is bypassed by the traffic racing along the road to Guisborough from Great Ayton, or vice-versa, and ignored by the energetic, set on climbing to the top of Cleveland's mini mountain, Roseberry Topping.

North Skelton 🖎

North Skelton is a mis-named village as it actually lies to the east of Skelton. The land here was originally called 'North Foggett', perhaps that is how the misnomer occurred.

The main village was built during the late 19th – early 20th centuries to house the workers from the ironstone mine, and to provide the necessary support services – school, shops etc. The majority of the homes are small terraced houses built along, and at right angles to, the main road which runs through the village. Additional modern housing, in the form of a small estate, was built on the outskirts in the 1970s.

The ironstone mine at North Skelton had a dual distinction. As drift-mining became less viable, the first deep shaft in the country was started here by Bolckow, Vaughan & Co in 1867 (its construction took three and a half years, and cost £100,000!). It was also the last mine to be closed when the seam finally ran out in January 1964. The mine-workers were originally drawn from the local population of agricultural labourers, but with the sinking of the deep shaft many aspects of the job became more technical and experienced men from the coal fields of Durham and the tin mines of Cornwall flocked to the area. Many brought their families with them, others inter-married with the indigenous population. Many Cornish names can still be found in the region today.

At first the winding gear was steam driven. Transportation of the ore at the seam was for many years horse-drawn – stables and smithy being part of the large underground complex. The horses were eventually replaced by steam power. Finally the diesel engine took over. In the early days of the mine, when a build up of inflammable gas was suspected, canaries were fetched from the Durham coal fields to test the atmosphere.

North Skelton is unusual in having two railway bridges crossing the main road within a few yards of each other. One carries the busy mineral line from Boulby Potash Mine to Saltburn. The other bore the now dismantled pit-head branch line. Now the mine yard and buildings are used by a light engineering firm. One of the few reminders of the past can be seen in the name of Bolckow Street.

The village hall is used for a number of ventures; East

Cleveland Village Arts is located there, it is used for practice sessions by North Skelton British Steel Band, and Social Services rent part of it as a day centre for the elderly of the village and surrounding areas.

The oldest inhabitant died recently, in her hundred and first year. She must have seen many changes, but the village, although almost joined to Skelton by modern housing, is still a lively community holding proudly to its separate identity.

Norton

A Bronze Age burial site is known to have existed on the Kendrews estate which lies to the east of the green. Norton House, the home of the Hogg family (Lord Hailsham the Lord Chancellor's family name) was demolished in the 1930s. The builders found stone coffins with daggers and other ornaments which they ordered to be covered in concrete. No one realised the significance of these finds at that time. Norton has kept its rural character over the years, despite the industrialisation that went on all around it.

The church at Norton dates from the late Saxon period. It became a collegiate church in 1081, to provide maintenance for a number of canons removed from Durham Cathedral because they refused to wear the habit of the monks. Thomas Sheraton, the great cabinet maker was married in St Mary's church. Evidence of his talent can be seen above the windows in the Unicorn inn near the green. John Claymond, vicar of Norton from 1498, was appointed in 1516 to be the first President of Corpus Christi College Oxford. He also founded a scholarship for a boy from Norton to go to Oxford University.

In 1099 a weekly market was granted to Norton, which

was held beside what is now the duck pond. A dew pond to the south of the church was established by tapping the many springs which flow under Norton. For 800 years this pond was the main fish and water supply to both the church and the villagers. The market ceased during the tumultuous years of the Civil War. Where the market cross stood is now Cross Dyke, which is even shown on modern maps. Dyke Pond became known as Duck Pond.

Over 280 years ago an elm tree was planted which became the focal point of the village green. It became known as the Jubilee Tree, but sadly it fell foul of Dutch elm disease and had to be felled on the morning of the 10th September 1987. The village and most of its activities centre around the green. At the north end of the High Street, formerly Front Street, was the forge, the Hamiltonian public house (now a news-agent's), a bakehouse, and the pinder's house. It was the pinder's job to see that the green was kept clean and tidy, and stray animals rounded up and secured behind his house, fines being levied against the owners before the animals were returned. The green was common land and legitimately used for grazing cattle. No pigs were allowed because they created too much damage.

North-west of the green is St Mary's church, and to the east is the Hermitage. Once a single storey building, it dates from the 11th century. Surrounding the green are many Georgian houses. The Friends meeting house was built in 1617. To the south-east was a tannery, the buildings are now used as a joinery.

By the 1800s houses were scattered all along Cross Dyke Lane and Calf Fallow Lane (now Junction Road and Station Road). The oldest building in Norton is The Priory, which was the home of the Bishop of Durham. This was a single storey building in 1100 and had a second storey added in Tudor times; brick and plaster was used in 1745 to update the building. Victorian houses were built all along the Stockton Road to the Lustrum Beck toll bridge. This bridge, originally a wooden structure was widened and rebuilt in stone sometime in the 18th century. Behind the High Street were many small dwellings, access to which was through gates from the High Street. Open land lay beyond these cottages. The gentlemen of Norton paid to have trees planted on the green in 1895.

Circa 1650 Norton grammar school was founded. 'The establishment consisted of twelve acres of land, cottages, and bakehouse for parishioners, besides a good house, containing the school room.' The income from the bakehouse went towards the upkeep of the school. The enclosure award to Norton in 1673 included a land grant to the school.

After the Education Act of 1870 Norton board school was built. Opened in 1873 it was demolished in 1983. The archway and clock from this school remain in the High Street, and are protected by a conservation order. The walkway beneath this arch is named Marbray King Walk, after the Speaker of the House of Commons (1965–1970) who was educated in Norton. There were various other small educational establishments in Norton, but by 1913 only one dame school survived.

A school for delicate children was set up in 1927, the first of its kind in the country. It was called the Open Air School. After six months of three meals a day and plenty of fresh air many of the children could return to a normal school. Later it was renamed Summer House School and catered for severely disabled children, then these pupils were admitted to ordinary schools and consequently this closed.

One of the legends passed down through the centuries is about Norton's buried treasure. During the Dissolution of the Monasteries in 1539, to forestall the church ormanents falling into the hands of the King, they were removed from

121

Durham Cathedral to be taken to Whitby via Norton. En route they heard of the fall of Whitby. The custodians of the treasure are reputed to have buried it to the east of the village, in such a way that they could recover it at a suitable time. It is believed that the church towers of Norton and Billingham were used as reference points. But where is the treasure now?

Another legend is about the ghostly hound of Blakestone, which unwittingly led a pack of hounds over the edge of a quarry to their doom. The ghost now appears to prevent such an accident happening again. Another ghost is reputedly the victim of a duel between two soldiers. The ghost, dressed in a black cloak, appears at the foot of the stairs at the Red Lion Hotel. The last sighting was reported in 1980.

Industry did have a place in Norton, even though it escaped the worst ravages of the industrialisation of the 19th century. A tannery existed on the green, and a glue factory on the Billingham Road. Market gardening and agriculture was the main source of income for the community. There were four mills, Bishop Mill and three others, still used in the mid 19th century. There was a blast furnace, a pottery and two breweries on a 30 acre site in Station Road. The bell for the clock (Big Ben) in the tower of the New Palace of Westminster was made at Norton blast furnace, transported by train to Hartlepool and then shipped to London. Upon its arrival it was tested and found to be perfect. Unfortunately there was a delay of 16 months before it was hung and then it was found to be cracked. Rumour says it was over-tested, but there was not sufficient time to send it back to Norton so it was re-cast at Whitechapel. Stockton Concrete Company opened next to Norton railway station. It made artificial stone sills for churches and paving stones. Norton Junction was one of the earliest railway systems in the country.

The Imperial Tramway Company bought two local com-

122

panies who had operated steam trams. In 1897 this company laid 15 miles of track in six months from Norton to North Ormesby. The last tram ran on the night of 31st December 1931. Also in 1931 the John Fox almshouses were built. They consist of twelve dwellings, a reading room and a caretaker's house and are set in gardens just off the High Street.

Cricket has been played on Norton Green from long before 1840. The minute book of the club founded in 1847 states that 'There is no place in the North of England where such a lively interest is taken in the national game of cricket, as in the village of Norton, the green being well fitted for the practice of the game, having ample space and being at all seasons perfectly dry.' Today the club has its own ground in Station Road. A medieval fair is now held once a year on the green, reviving old customs.

The appearance of the High Street and its properties has changed little over the centuries. The Conservation Society, the custodians of Norton's past, are preserving it for the future.

Nunthorpe 🌿

Until the mid 19th century and the industrialisation of Teesside, Nunthorpe consisted of Nunthorpe village and a small but properous farming community, within the parish of Great Ayton. There was an old Hall with its own domestic chapel and home farm, and on the other side of the road was a row of houses, a smithy, but no inn. It was a very secluded community.

In the Domesday Book the village is called Thorp, a Saxon

name meaning a small settlement near a large one, Great Ayton. Thorp was the name until the nuns settled here in the 12th century. The nuns, not the best behaved despite the records showing that they came from distinguished families, upset the community so much that the prefix Nun stuck to Thorp, and created the name Nunthorpe.

Adam de Brus, lord of the manor, gave permission for the founding of a nunnery at Hutton Lowcross in 1162, close to Guisborough Priory. The convent consisted of a prioress and eight or nine nuns. While at Hutton Lowcross the nuns quarrelled and were such a nuisance to their neighbours that they had to leave, and were resettled at Nunthorpe. Along with the land they had a small priory and a mill. The site of this priory is not known. Nunthorpe Hall or Grange Farm are possible locations. It is rumoured that a ghost of a nun walks in the grounds of Nunthorpe Hall.

The nuns were not long in their new home before their behaviour brought down the wrath of the ecclesiastical authorities. They decided to send the offending nuns to live in 'Basedale'. Baysdale is a secluded valley at the end of Westerdale. This did not improve their behaviour. Horse stealing was added to their list of 'crimes'.

Nunthorpe is credited with having a resident warlock. He was evil and one-eyed. Richard Blakeborough in his book *Yorkshire Wit, Character and Custom*, relates the story of how he lost his eye. It is a tale of incantations under a rowan tree, fire at midnight and the making of a wax image by one of the warlock's victims, all under the supervision of the Wiseman of Stokesley. The story ends with 'when the fire died down the ashes were buried in the churchyard'. The wax figure removed from the mould was pierced with two small holes to represent the eyes. The victim of the warlock made an incantation, pressed a pin into the eye of the model and pronounced the spell complete. The victim found that all his pain left him as he walked home. The warlock of Nunthorpe awoke with only one sighted eye.

Great changes came to the area when the railway was built in 1853. The first line carried iron ore from the Guisborough mines to Middlesbrough. Very quickly other lines radiated throughout the area. Isaac Wilson, a Quaker, director of the railways and a founding father of Middlesbrough, lived at Nunthorpe Hall. He was the first chairman of the Tees Conservancy Board and under his direction the sand-choked Tees was changed into a navigable waterway. He was the second Mayor, and the second Member of Parliament for Middlesbrough. Nunthorpe, still in a rural setting, became the 'uppercrust' residential area for Cleveland. During the latter part of the 19th century Nunthorpe station was a very busy junction, and remained so until the Beeching axe fell.

Isaac Wilson was an old man when another ironmaster came to live at Nunthorpe, at Grey Towers, which became Poole Hospital, Arthur Dorman. He had a profound effect on the iron and steel industry of Teesside, but also on Nunthorpe. Before the First World War he had built houses for his workforce. These were very different from the working class terraces of Middlesbrough. They were in terraces of six or more, with large rooms and three or four bedrooms, in tree-lined avenues. He also decreed that there would be no shops, no slated roofs and no public houses. Even today these are very desirable houses. He built a school and the schoolmaster's house (now the vicarage). With Temple Moore as the architect he was the moving force behind the building of the parish church in fine Gothic style.

The community gradually jelled and together they created a fund to buy a large army hut which became known as the Institute. It was used by the men as a billiard hall and to play chess while the women held their WI meetings. All the village activities took place in this hall, but no alcohol was allowed.

The centre of the community, 70 years later it is still the only community centre. Nunthorpe also has a very fine Methodist church built in 1911 which replaced an older chapel.

Sir Arthur Dorman, a keep sportsman, allowed cricket matches to be played in the grounds of his home, Grey Towers. Public tennis courts were made in Rookwood Road, and surprisingly Nunthorpe had a polo ground. In 1906 Lady Harrison bought this ground and donated it to the community for a cricket pitch. It is now the sports field with squash courts and a well appointed licensed pavilion.

In 1931 Alderman Poole bought Grey Towers and gave it to the town of Middlesbrough as a sanitorium for the care of TB patients. Research carried on here eventually led to the cure of this disease. Latterly used as a geriatric hospital it is now closed and its future is uncertain.

Rampant development after the Second World War means Nunthorpe is now a suburb of Middlesbrough. There are shops, banks, a post office and all modern amenities. On the south side Nunthorpe is still recognisable as the rural village of Isaac Wilson.

Ormesby

The Saxon lord of the manor, Orme, was replaced by Robert de Brus just after the Norman Conquest. He was followed by the Percys of Northumberland, and then in the 16th century by the Pennymans who retained Ormesby until the death of Colonel J. B. Pennyman in 1961, when it was bequeathed to the National Trust.

The church of St Cuthbert is a modern building on ancient foundations. Saxon and Danish sculptures have been found in the churchyard. A bequest from Miss C. Brown of

Ormesby House provided the means in 1905 to erect a tower and spire, and eight bells dedicated to the Northern saints. When the floor of the vestry was found to be unsafe Cleveland archaeologists excavated and found a Viking cross, which has been dated circa AD 950. A little stream runs through the churchyard.

Ormesby vicarage is reputed to be, or at least partly to be, one of the oldest buildings in the area. One outside wall is possibly a thousand years old. When the building was extended Roman coins of Septimus Severus were found. They were sent to York, but unfortunately they were lost in a bombing raid on that city in the Second World War. These coins were not the only treasure found at the vicarage. When the house was under repair in the 19th century, an ancient wooden box was found in an enclosed cavity in one of the walls. It contained coinage from the reigns of Henry VI, Edward VI, Henry VII and Henry VIII. They were claimed as treasure trove. It is believed that this treasure had been removed from Guisborough Priory just before the Dissolution of the Monasteries. It is known that the Prior from Guisborough spent some time at Ormesby vicarage just after the priory was dissolved.

Ormesby Hall was the seat of the Pennyman family for three and a half centuries. James Pennyman bought the manor of Ormesby in 1600. Despite all the political and religious upheavals of the time the Pennymans prospered. Staunch Royalists, the Pennymans were severely fined by the Commonwealth government. The third James Pennyman was knighted in the field of battle for bravery. Upon the Restoration of the Monarchy he was rewarded with a baronetcy. His son became Lord Privy Seal to William III, and the High Sheriff of Yorkshire in 1702.

In Ormesby High Street is the old school house dated 1744, also a row of almshouses which are over 200 years old. Unfortunately the old village inn and some old cottages were demolished when the new pub and shopping centre were built.

Ormesby Hall is open to the public through the auspices of the National Trust. The stables, possibly designed by John Carr of York are now used by the mounted police to house their horses. Ormesby is certainly considerably larger than the 305 persons recorded in 1808. The houses spread in all directions and it is difficult to differentiate between the many villages that lay to the south of Middlesbrough and have now been swallowed up by that sprawling conurbation.

Pinchinthorpe

Pinchinthorpe is a small village south-west of Guisborough and situated in the National Park. It consists of a few scattered farms, some houses, the Hall and Pinchinthorpe House. Pinchinthorpe comprises lowland, hill slopes, some moorland and Forestry Commission land. The name Pinchinthorpe is derived from a Norman–French family, Pinchin. Originally it was called Thorpe. In Guisborough churchyard is a gravestone, engraved William Frank of Thorpe. In the 19th century Thorpe was prefixed with Pinchin.

Pinchinthorpe Hall is an attractive gabled house with imposing garden walling. It was originally surrounded by a moat. In the late 16th century it became the home of the Lee family. During the Civil War William Lee's horse was stolen by the Royalists. The King ordered it to be returned. In the 17th and 18th centuries the building was enlarged and improved. In 1836 after the tragic suspected suicide of John Lee, the Lee family left the Hall. It was occupied by tenants until the Lees sold the estate.

The Peases of Hutton Hall had been gradually buying up land in the Pinchinthorpe area, but never managed to buy the Hall and its accompanying estate. Sir Joseph Pease, however, leased the Hall for 30 years, and during that time made some improvements to the place. The next tenant was Percy Williams and the Hall was connected to the Williams family until 1987. Today, it is said that the Hall is going to be developed commercially.

Pinchinthorpe House is Victorian and was created from two farms, one of which was called Spout House. It came into the ownership of the Thomas family. Henry William Thomas was an extrovert personality who was not satisfied with the old farm houses, he renamed them Pinchinthorpe House. Later it became the home of Sir Alfred Pease. The house was altered and quite considerably enlarged. Part of the buildings became a chapel. During the Second World War the Debenhams took over the house.

Pinchinthorpe station was opened in the late 1850s. The station houses built in 1871 are now a private house. The Old Road leading down to the station had a level crossing. In 1876 the station was re-sited on the other side of the road and a bridge was built to replace the crossing. A branch line from Chaloner Pit joined the main line at Pinchinthorpe about 1872. The station was closed in 1951, but the railway line remained open until 1964.

Lowcross Farm is considered to be the site of the medieval leper hospital. The farm, always important in the area, has, situated on the opposite side of the road, an 18th century barn which was used as the tithe barn; '1751' and 'T. B.' are etched on the wall. The Thomas family lived at Lowcross Farm until the 1840s.

The total area of Pinchinthorpe is approximately one and a half square miles. It is a very pleasant area and only a few new houses have been built in the last 30 years.

Preston-upon-Tees 🦜

The original parish of Preston stands on the north side of the river Tees at the point where the celebrated Whinstone Dyke passes through the area and crosses the river. At this point it is 75 ft wide and has been quarried to a considerable depth, although no quarrying has taken place for many years. It is bounded on one side by the river and on the other by the railway.

The parish of Preston is mentioned in church records of 1025 when it was referred to as church lands. It appears to have been composed mainly of scattered farms and possibly a small hamlet. The population at the end of the 14th century was 45 and in 1911 it had grown to 618 with 212 houses. Today however most of these houses are deemed to be part of the adjoining village of Eaglescliffe.

Its main claim to fame locally is its connection with the original Stockton to Darlington Railway line for which Stockton-on-Tees Borough Council are currently setting up a Railway Heritage Trail. In the grounds of Preston Park a pathway runs parallel with the main Yarm road and a plaque placed upon it states that it is the route of the original trackbed of the Stockton to Darlington Railway. It ran through the grounds of Preston Hall (built 1825) until about 1852, when the Leeds Northern Railway was built along the present line a quarter of a mile away.

There was trouble between the owner of the Hall, David Burton Fowler, and the railway when sparks from a locomotive damaged saplings on the estate. It was probably also here that Locomotion, hauling the opening day's train on 27th September 1825, ran its legendary race with a stage-coach on nearby Yarm Road.

Because the line was moved, Preston Junction was closed and the new station which was built to service the new line was named Eaglescliffe and the development which grew up around it, although much of it is still in the parish of Preston-upon-Tees, the area took on the name of the new station. If things had happened differently, then Preston-upon-Tees might well have been the name of this now sprawling residential area. Today all that remains bearing its name is Preston Hall Museum and Park, a single row of houses bordering the park known as Preston Lane and an unusual feature called Moorhouse Farm Estate.

In 1820 David Burton Fowler acquired land at Preston and built Preston Hall, which was completed in 1825. In 1882 it was bought by Sir Robert Ropner, a local shipbuilder, who modernised and enlarged the building, adding the conservatory and stone porch and moving the entrance to its present position from what is now the rear of the building.

In 1937 the last Ropner died and the Hall was leased to Ashmore Benson & Pease Ltd, who used it as offices for a time. A plan to demolish it and build a housing estate failed due to building restrictions after the Second World War. It was eventually acquired by Stockton Borough Council who opened it as a museum in 1953. The extensive grounds form Preston Park and both facilities are widely used.

In the early 1970s a search of the attics in Preston Hall brought to light a number of treasures among a collection of paintings known as the Clepham Bequest, left to the council by a local family in 1930. As well as two Lowrys and a Turner entitled *Mustering of the Warrior Angels*, a painting by Georges de la Tour was discovered. There are apparently only 34 of his paintings in existence and the only other one in this country is in the Queen's collection at Hampton Court. Entitled *The Dice Players*, it was valued at a quarter of a million pounds at that time and now hangs in the museum under strict security. The museum also houses the Spence Bequest, an extensive collection of arms and armour.

131

In recent years the museum has added a toy gallery, costume collection, reconstructed rooms of the Georgian, Edwardian and Victorian periods and a transport museum. It also holds many items connected with the history of Stockton-on-Tees, Stockton Castle and the surrounding areas. The most ambitious recent addition is a reconstruction of a late 19th century shopping street and craft galleries where farriers, blacksmiths and workers in wood can be seen in action during the summer months.

The Moorhouse Farm Estate consists of a double row of houses isolated in the middle of fields. There appears to be no reason for their existence, in the middle of nowhere, but it seems that they were built in 1936 as a result of the Land Settlement Act. This was a project to redeploy unemployed miners and steelworkers etc. during the depression.

After a short training period in agriculture and small animal husbandry, those considered to be suitable were rented a house and several acres of land in a cooperative smallholding venture. They raised pigs, produced eggs and vegetables which were sold to the Stockton Cooperative Society and at local markets. A Dutchman was brought over to teach the men cold glasshouse horticulture, growing otherwise unobtainable vegetables such as tomatoes, cucumbers, lettuce etc. This was a great success as they grew and marketed 4,000 pounds of tomatoes in the first season. Many of the men became accomplished smallholders and were never unemployed again.

This is the one time in history that men have been taken from the towns to the country in a time of high unemployment. County Durham (as this area then was) was the only area of the country to take full advantage of this government scheme which took 7,000 men off the unemployment register.

Moorhouse is just one of the 304 such estates established under the scheme and remains as a reminder of the ideal behind it, although the Second World War and full employment brought an end to the scheme and the houses are now privately owned and the land resold to local farms. As building encroaches on this isolated group of houses from both directions, it will, no doubt soon no longer be the oddity it is today.

A large new industrial estate is now taking shape on land in Preston parish, to be called the Preston Farm Estate, after the farm to which the land belonged. Ironic in view of the fact that farming is becoming less and less the industry of the area.

Redmarshall 🌿

In the first half of the 20th century Redmarshall was one of the smallest villages in County Durham. The church built in the 12th century is on the same site as an earlier Saxon church. St Cuthbert's body rested here on its long wandering before finally being laid to rest at Durham Cathedral. Within the church are the recumbent effigies of Sir Thomas Langton and his wife Sybil, formerly lord and lady of the manor. One of the features of Redmarshall church is the leper window. This was used when the lepers from the nearby colony came to the church to receive communion. This leper colony was housed on the land that is now known as Glebe Farm.

Standing to the north-east of the church is the old rectory. Built in the Victorian era, it bears a plaque which states, 'Reverend Austin 1845'. This gentleman raised 14 children in this house, twelve of whom survived into adulthood.

It is reputed there was a tunnel, or some form of escape

route running from the church to Castle Hill at Bishopton almost two miles in length, Castle Hill supposedly being built from the surplus soil. Actually the mound is a fine example of a late Norman motte and bailey castle.

During the Second World War the rectory was used as a haven for evacuees from the Blitz in London. Land Girls were working on the farms at Redmarshall. This meagre workforce was supplemented by prisoners of war of many nationalities, but predominantly Italian, helping in the nation's effort to 'Dig For Victory'.

Adjacent to the rectory is Rose House Farm, and situated in the farmyard is one of the only two wheelsheds surviving in the area. These were used in the grinding of corn; a horse was tethered to a long shaft protruding from the central wheel, as the horse walked around and around it turned the shaft that turned the wheel which ground the wheat. Rose Farm is obviously the site of many generations of farming as the ancient ridge and furrows are, despite modern farming methods, still visible in the surrounding fields. Only two of the original four farms survive at Redmarshall, and in the current decline in farming a question mark must be raised about their survival.

Redmarshall is said to have acquired its name from the reed marshes and bogs that exist in the area. The Ship inn is the only public house in the village. It has changed hands many times over the years, but none of the owners could have been more colourful than the landlady who was reputed to be a contortionist, and revealed her talents to a 'privileged' few.

In recent years the village school has not only been closed but completely demolished, not a brick remains. A bungalow now occupies this site in Church Lane. Opposite stands a nursing home which was one of the original farms.

The village of Redmarshall is situated between Darlington

and Stockton, formerly in the County of Durham, now in Cleveland. From being the smallest village, the post-war boom in building and population has ensured that this title is no longer viable. No longer a rural population, the present inhabitants commute to various locations for their work, but are cosmopolitan in origin and attitude.

Seaton Carew 🦡

During the excavations for the foundations for Hartlepool nuclear power station, situated at Seaton Carew, fragments of human bones, deer, plus the remains of trees last living in the Stone Age 6,000–2,000 years ago, were brought to the surface by the mechanical excavators. Between Seaton and Hartlepool, Roman pottery and coins have been discovered, possibly evidence that the Romans had a fort here. Little surface evidence remains of the many Norse invaders. This is not surprising because this stretch of the coast is subject to erosion, which has been somewhat alleviated by the building of the Hartlepool harbour and the breakwater at the Tees estuary.

During the reign of Henry I, Seaton was held by Robert de Carrowe. It was at this time that Seaton became Seaton Carrowe and later Seaton Carew. A chapel was built here in 1200 at the request of Peter de Carrowe. The chapel, dedicated to Thomas a Becket, was licensed by the Prior of Durham. Peter de Carrowe had to pay Guisborough Priory 60 acres of land which had pasture for 100 ewes, plus their lambs and three cottages. The chapel was serviced by a canon from Guisborough Priory. This arrangement lasted until the Dissolution of the Monasteries. This chapel was completely ruined by 1622. Today there are no visible

135

remains, possibly they were all washed out to sea with the continual erosion.

Seaton Carew was in the parish of Stranton, and Stranton churchyard was the last resting place for the people of Seaton. John Wesley stopped at Seaton, and held services for the population in the kitchen of the cottage where he stayed. The Bishop of Durham, Robert de Sitchel gave land from Seaton to Merton College Oxford when it was founded in 1264.

Salt making has always been a viable operation in the salt marshes surrounding Seaton Carew. Salt, made by evaporation in ancient times, was still processed in the same way in the 19th century.

When visiting the seaside became popular with the gentry, the wide expanse of land at Seaton Carew attracted many visitors (circa 1750). They arrived by stagecoach. By the 19th century and the advent of the railways, three quarters of the population at Seaton was involved in the tourist trade. A hotel was built for the upper crust of society. It had a large ballroom with a gallery for the orchestra. All important social functions were held there. There were many other forms of accommodation for the visitor from large boarding houses to small cottages taking in a single lodger.

As you can expect the turbulent North Sea periodically gives a display of its awesome power. Thirty three vessels were washed up on the beach in a storm in 1785. A gentleman from Darlington presented Seaton with a lifeboat in 1804. Water poured through the streets of Seaton Carew after another fierce storm in 1836.

Trinity church and its parsonage was built in 1831 and a burial ground in 1842. No records remain of a school before the Church school was opened in 1844.

William Gray, the ship builder from West Hartlepool, purchased 100 acres of land near to Seaton Carew. They established a shipyard and built houses for their workers and named it Graythorp. During the First World War they built a dry dock and this kept going through the slump of the 1930s. It was closed in 1968. The discovery of oil and gas in the North Sea brought changes to the area. Graythorpe was taken over by Laing Offshore in 1972. They have gained world wide recognition for the construction of giant oil rigs.

The salt marshes surrounding Seaton Carew attract thousands of migratory birds as they journey north or south, depending on the species and the time of year. Arctic seals can be seen resting on the sand banks all the year.

Although high tides can cause widespread problems and disasters, abnormally low tides are known to occur, and when this happens it reveals the remains of a primeval forest that existed 4,000 years ago, which stretched from Britain to Scandinavia.

In 1948 it was suggested that wind erosion of the dunes could be checked by the planting of brushwood across the sand. In 1990 the local authorities asked the people to donate their used Christmas trees to be planted on the beach. Rootless, they will not grow, but they have all been planted and the conservationists are optimistic that they will retain and build up a large wall of sand. What will the archaeologists think if they dig this unnatural forest up in 200 or 300 years time?

Skelton

Skelton in Cleveland is a village with a long and chequered history. During the reign of Edward the Confessor it was the manor of Uctred the Saxon; in 1086 the lands were owned by the Count of Mortain. William I gave them to one of his knights, Robert de Brus. Robert, his son, had a 240 ft wide moat dug, and the excavated earth was used to form the 'great and lofty eminence' on which he built a stone castle.

The names of the lords of the manor of Skelton have changed several times in the last 900 years, though only once by sale. They have passed several times by female inheritance (leading, on one occasion, to a severe family feud, when the interior of the castle – including the beautiful chapel 'a jewel in the kingdom's crown' – was wrecked by all four claimants, to prevent their rivals benefiting). One owner died in the Tower, for debt; two were declared insane and unfit to inherit. Through de Bruses, Fauconbergs, Conyers, Frotters, Stevensons and Whartons, the lands have passed. The present owner still lives at the castle, opening the grounds once a year for charity, on Daffodil Sunday.

Today's castle contains only minimal remains of the original building. Much of it was rebuilt in 1330, it was repaired again in 1339 and only ten years later was described as 'expensive to maintain'. By 1490 it was 'ruinous and of no value'. Oliver Cromwell passed close by. The castle is situated in a vale, closely surrounded by the remnants of the hunting forest of the de Bruses; it was not visible from the high ground. The soldiers failed to see it and moved on. The villagers rejoiced, too loudly! The troops heard them, turned back and soundly defeated them at the battle of Flowston Hill. This small skirmish does not rate a mention in the history books, but is part of the folk-memory of the community.

During the 18th century the owner, John Hall Stevenson, friend of Lawrence Sterne (author of *Tristram Shandy*) and founder of the local Hell Fire Club, entertained lavishly in his 'Crazy Castle', despite its run-down condition. Destruction came in 1788, when his grandson, another John (who assumed the name of Wharton), demolished the old castle, pulled down the man-made hill on which it stood and filled in the huge moat. In 1794 he had built a Gothic-style, castellated mansion, fronted by a lake. This is the Skelton Castle of today.

We know much of the lords of the manor, little of the ordinary people. All that remains of the medieval village is an old well-head on Spout Hill; what was probably the whipping post, on what is left of the village green; and the drovers' road called Boroughgate Lane, with its ancient stone drinking troughs.

The borough (site uncertain, but probably well away from the estate village), was never very prosperous during its 400 year existence. The well-being of all in the area depended to a great extent upon the patronage of their lord. Even in modern times great landowners can have considerable influence. The Whartons have done much for the area.

In the 18th century, the first of that name built a school for the village and gave land for a chapel. When, a hundred years later, ironstone mining came to the area and new villages were being built and old ones extended, they provided sites for churches and institutes. The New Skelton of Victorian days was built beyond the eastern end of the High Street, with houses, school, chapel, Salvation Army hall and many shops. The rise in population was dramatic. Between 1861 and 1881 numbers increased from just over 1,000 to almost eight times that figure. As the first flush of ironstone mining-fever faded, as labour-intensive drift mining and deep-shaft sinking ended, fewer workers were needed. Unemployment hit the area. In 1884 some 1,500 people (a few families but mainly single men) emigrated from the immediate area to America.

Religious feelings were very strong in the 19th century. In 1813 Thomas Wharton gave the Wesleyans land on which to build a chapel. When the Primitive Methodists split away and wanted to erect their own meeting house, he disappro-

139

ved and refused, finally selling them the land at a high price. Money was short; the clay was donated and one of their members (in his own time, and after regularly working a ten hour day) made each of the 30,000 bricks needed. It flourished from 1865 until 1940, when the breech was finally healed, and can be seen today near the bottom of Green Road. A few yards to the south stands the West End Methodist chapel, built in 1877 on land donated by Mr Wharton. This classical-style building was designed to seat 700; at the back is a schoolroom and caretaker's house, originally there was also stabling for the minister's horse.

The Anglican community was building too. Glebe land, sold for £7,400, paid for much of the new Gothic-style parish church, built 1881–84. The tower, its clock and peal of six bells, were the gift of Mr J. T. Wharton. In the early 1920s, Col W. H. A. Wharton gave the stained glass west window as a memorial to the dead of the First World War. The small Christ-figure on the wooden cross in the Lady chapel was picked up on the battlefield of Ypres. At the back of the church is a 13th century bell, originally in Skelton Old Church.

This church was erected in 1325 close to the castle. It replaced an earlier foundation, and part of a sundial bearing Anglo–Saxon lettering, but in the Old Norse language, was unearthed nearby. It is now incorporated in the porch of the New Church. Three coffins of late Saxon/early Norman origin were found here. For about a hundred years a weekly market was held in the churchyard, after the Sunday morning service, until, in 1321, it was changed to a Saturday and a larger, more suitable market place was found.

Almost the only remnant of the Norman church is a large slab of blue marble set into the chancel floor. This is believed to be a Fauconberg memorial, but the brasses are missing. The church was pulled down and a new building erected in

1785. It is a beautiful example of 18th century ecclesiastical architecture, with its triple-decker pulpit, west gallery and enclosed pews. Skelton Old Church was closed in 1904. After standing empty for over 80 years it was lovingly restored and services are now held there three times a year.

Of the Victorian settlement only a few terraces remain. A new New Skelton mushroomed in the 1960s and 1970s to the north and east of the main village. Here, on the housing estates, are shops and schools, a recreation ground and industrial estate, health centre and sheltered housing, library and civic hall.

Skelton is now too large to retain a true village atmosphere, but it is still a friendly place. Varied social and voluntary activities draw people together. A newcomer showing willing to put down roots and take an active part in village life, is sure of a genuine welcome.

Skelton Green 🐚

Skelton Green is an ironstone mining village on high ground to the south of, and almost joined to, Skelton.

In early medieval times it was the site of an important crossroads. The north/south route linked the de Brus estates of Marske and Skelton, along the drove road by Boosbeck, to their holdings at Danby, thence over the moors to Malton and York. The west/east road was the 'via de Witebi'. This went from Guisborough, over Airy Hill, roughly followed the present line of Trout Hall Lane, then almost due east to the coast with which it curved towards Whitby.

A charter of 1292 refers to a street called 'Pottersty' running along the top of Airy Hill. Nearby was 'Kiln Nook Gate'. References to the potter's craft appear in various records for the next hundred years. In 1969 Skelton WEA held a 'dig' in the area. They turned up many pieces of 12th–14th century pottery and evidence of some early habitation, but failed to locate 'the lost borough of Skelton'. A bulletin on this subject was issued, in 1971, by the Cleveland and Teesside Local History Society. This detailed the history of the market, granted by charter to the de Bruses in the late 12th century, and of the borough of craftsmen, tradesmen and merchants which was established near this market place and was in existence for some 400 years.

The society points to several possible sites, but concludes that the evidence available strongly suggests that they were not an integral part of the estate village of Skelton, but were founded some half mile to the south. They believe that the market was probably held on Manless Green (the very name indicates a once used, but later abandoned, site of some kind). This was the large, roughly triangular area of 'waste' at the top of Market Street (now Green Road), where the estate's drove road and the via de Witebi crossed; the open land on which, in the late 1800s, the main part of the mining village was built. A short distance away, to the west, Boroughgate Lane makes a right-angled turn to join Manless Green. It is on the area of 'waste' in this angle that the local historians suggest that the commercial borough probably existed.

Maps from the late 16th century onwards, all show a few dwellings scattered around Manless Green; one of these always being at the apex of the triangle. Some 50 years before the mining village was built, this prime site was occupied by the Green inn. Altered, extended and closely crowded by turn of the century buildings, it is one of the two remaining public houses in the village today.

It is not clear when the name Skelton Green came into official usage. In Kelly's Directory of 1937, it is only used for the streets to the east of Boosbeck Road. This road and the built-up area to the west is called High Green. The area is shown as an integral part of the village of Skelton; it is not even a separate ward.

It was, however, much more of a true village than it is today. There was a miners' hospital (owned and maintained by Col Wharton of Skelton Castle, and boasting two surgeons as well as a full nursing staff), a school, a chapel, an institute (now being saved from dereliction, and converted for use by the Jehovah's Witnesses), a sub-post office, three public houses, and numerous small shops providing all daily necessities.

A life-long resident remembers the days when the women gathered to gossip round the pump in Park Street; when miners' wives, in clean white aprons, stood on their freshly scrubbed doorsteps awaiting their husbands' return, with the all-important pay-packet, on a Friday evening. Life was hard, danger in the mine was an ever present fear, but these facts of life led to a very close-knit community.

The school and hospital are now gone, and almost all of the shops. Gone too are the old village characters; Bill Buck playing darts in the Miners Arms; Mrs Bowgen the 'layer-out'; Ron Easton, farmer and village poet, whose gate bore the warning:

'Be ye man or be ye woman,
Be ye gannin' or be ye comin',
Be ye early or be ye late,
Den't forget to close the gate.'

In the late 1960s Langbaurgh Council declared the houses of Harker Street, Cleveland Street and Park Street unfit for modernisation. The residents fought long and hard, but were finally moved to a new estate in Skelton, and almost 120 houses were demolished. New houses have been, and are

143

being, built. There is still much open space where the old terraces stood.

Most people now work, shop, and find their relaxation outside the immediate area. 'Incomers' say that there is a 'wonderful village atmosphere' and that neighbours become close friends. Those who remember the past, say that it is now a place of tiny cliques, no longer a whole community. What of the future? Will Skelton Green become a commuter village, or will it one day have a central life of its own again?

Stainsby ❧

This deserted medieval village lies between Thornaby and Acklam. The name means Stein's Hamlet and suggests a pre-Conquest settlement and it is mentioned in the Domesday Book. Stainsby beck runs by this hamlet.

It is known that they practised some form of fish farming. Both Guisborough Priory and Bylands Abbey are recorded as having an interest in the fishery in 1247. Old maps denote a church here, but there are no visible remains of such a structure. There are no records of residents after 1757, so possibly Stainsby was the victim of enclosure.

In 1969 this archaeological site was the first in Britain to have the proposed route of a major road (A19) diverted to preserve it.

Stainton & Thornton ❧

Stainton means place of stone and there has been a quarry here since Norman times. The stone seam, the Great Whin Sill stretches from Whitby in the south to Durham in the north and even across the sea to Ireland. Before the Norman Conquest the manor of Stainton included Acklam, Thornton, Hemlington, Ingleby Barwick, Thornaby and the farms at Stainsby. It is mentioned in the Domesday Book that Stainton was among the lands of Robert Mallet. Later the manor of Stainton was given to Robert de Brus, and then through marriage to Marmaduke de Thweng, followed by the Meynells and Sir William Pennyman. The last owner of the Grange was Major Dickins, whose mother-in-law was Lady Fawcett.

Stainton has had a church for over a thousand years. The first was most probably built of wood. The present church of St Peter and St Paul is built of sandstone. Incorporated in an outside wall is a Saxon cross and a 9th century 'hogback', the end piece of a Norse chieftain's memorial. The church was renovated in Victorian times. Inside there are several inscriptions to the Pennyman family. The WI window, donated in 1972, marked 100 years of service to the parish, and was in loving memory of William and Lady Adeline Fawcett. The parish records contain the signatures of the parents of Captain James Cook who were married in this church circa 1720.

When Sir William Fawcett died, the children from the village school were allowed to go and watch the funeral procession. His coffin was covered in the Union Jack, and the glass topped carriage was drawn along by matching shire horses, bedecked in funeral black and shining brasses.

The two villages of Stainton and Thornton sit astride Stainton beck. This beck flows from east to west, with Stainton on the north bank and Thornton on the south. They are connected by a road which dips as it passes over Kellgate Bridge. Stainton village is star-shaped, radiating out from the crossroads with the village green at its centre. Thornton is T-shaped, built around a road junction.

In 1968 when Teesside County Borough was formed, Stainton Parish Council was dissolved. It had existed since 1894 when councils had been set up throughout the land. To fill the gap in the villagers' civic affairs, Stainton and Thornton Residents Association was formed. They worked closely with Cleveland County Council. With the formation of Stainton and Thornton Parish Council in 1986, the Residents Association was disbanded.

There was a considerable increase in house building after the Second World War. In 1974 the oldest parts of the two villages were designated conservation areas, with several of the buildings being listed of historical or architectural importance. Two estates, totalling 150 houses, were built on land vacated by the closure of the old school (1876) and an engineering workshop. Adjacent to this site is the old whinstone quarry which is being developed as a nature conserva-

Stainton Village

tion area. In Thornton a redundant nursery garden site provided the land for 15 larger domestic properties.

Stainton is fortunate to have retained its post office and small general store. There is also a newsagent/winestore, and a hairdresser's with a wool shop. The development of Hemlington and Coulby Newham used some of the agricultural land for the building of access roads. Stainton and Thornton are still surrounded by five farms, and good open spaces. The local services are well maintained under the vigilant eye of the parish council.

The 13th century church and church hall, the Methodist chapel (1840), the Stainton Memorial Hall (1844) and the Stainton Hotel (1897) are the nucleus of the village community's social life. The old National school is now an architect's office, children of the village go to Hemlington for their schooling. Stainton House, a listed Georgian vicarage, is a British Steel conference centre.

The 900th anniversary celebration of the Domesday Book was marked with a festival. A collection of memorabilia, from the earliest times to 1986 was placed in a capsule and buried for posterity. Currently there is a history project to produce a booklet for newcomers and visitors. The villages are also involved in the nationwide 'Parish Maps' (Common Ground) project.

The Memorial (village) Hall was successively used as a school, a church hall, and by the first parish council. The hall caters for many activities, including those of the WI, the parish council, whist and bridge clubs, carpet bowling, art and crafts group, garden society, a small theatrical group, and the popular Saturday coffee mornings. The excellent gardens, well kept villages and open spaces encouraged villagers to enter the 'Britain in Bloom' competition from 1974. They have won several prizes, including the All-England 'Best Rose Village' 1976, and the Northumbria in

Bloom 'Best Large Village' 1988. The parish council has resurrected the village water pump and plans a village pond.

There is a residential nursing home for the elderly. Between Stainton and Hemlington is Larchfield Community, an offshoot of the Camphill Village Trust, which provides a home and work for mentally handicapped adults in agriculture and crafts activities.

Whilst accepting some modernisation and expansion, it is the aim to retain Stainton and Thornton's village character, which has survived for a thousand years.

Stillington

Few visitors to Stillington today can visualise what life was like here in the past. Most visitors are surprised to find industry in such an unlikely place, providing a variety of work requiring a high degree of skill and precision – an irregular group of workshops planted in an out of the way Victorian village in a rural setting, with many relics of the past all around.

The huge slag heap that used to dominate the village has been removed. In the past it would light up the whole village when red hot molten residue from the ironworks furnaces was tipped on the heap at night time. Removed in 1960, much of the slag was used in the making of the A1 motorway in County Durham. The old blacking mill has gone, which belched forth clouds of black dust which attached itself to trees, houses and workers. It has been replaced by a workshop that specialises in metallic insulation for nuclear reactors which are made under clinically clean conditions. The glycerine factory is also a thing of the past. It used to produce grease blocks used in the rolling mills. To make the blocks the material was boiled and it produced the most obnoxious smell that permeated the whole area. This factory, built of wood, took only 15 minutes to burn down to the ground in 1955. It was rebuilt to produce paint and paint brushes, but closed in 1960. Stillite products came to Stillington in 1939. After the slump of the early 1930s it brought much needed employment to the village. Industry was established at Stillington in the 1860s when Samuel Boston founded the Carlton Iron Works.

There were only three cottages prior to the founding of the Carlton Iron Works. One hundred and eleven houses were built in Lawson and Morris Streets, with a Co-operative store, the Argyll fish shop, and Calverts the general dealers. These were all demolished and the people were rehoused in another part of the village. Now the housing is a mixture of old and new, council and private, and some provided by the companies for their workforce.

The first school in the village was established in Cassidi Hall; its head master was Thomas Fenton and the school opened in January 1875. He was the only teacher for 90 children. In 1878 there were three teachers, but the pupils had increased to 170. An epidemic of measles in 1880 resulted in the school being closed for three weeks. The county council were responsible for the school from 1904 and the reports of the school were appalling.

In 1911 the new school was built on the site where the present school now stands. During the 1920s illness still disrupted school life, but there was a marked improvement in the 1930s. Art and music became an important part of school life and they produced their first play in 1938. Frequent air-raids in the Second World War disrupted classes, and the children spent a lot of time in the shelters. From 1960 children of secondary age went to school in Sedgefield. Lawson infant school was closed and the pupils transferred to what is now known as Stillington Junior Mixed and Infants School. A service was held in St John's church to celebrate the centenary of the school in 1975.

Another milestone in the history of the school was the amalgamation with Wynyard Church school in 1985. The new school is called The William Cassidi Church of England school, commemorating the first school in the Cassidi Hall. The school today has a high reputation, a fitting tribute to all those that laboured, in adverse conditions, to educate the children of yesteryear.

Stillington village is a thriving, bustling place, well kept and proud of its heritage. It has a fish shop, hairdresser's, post office, newsagent's and general store, a working men's club, a pub, a thriving village hall, the former Lawson Street school, tennis courts, cricket field, football field, quoits pitches, and a shooting range. A billiard centre, senior citizens club, bowls club, leek club, youth club, bingo nights and church fetes make up a busy schedule of events. The medical centre is a superb modern building designed by a local architect from Carlton.

The rise of modern industries in Stillington has turned the clock full circle. Whereas the railways and the ironworks created the Victorian industrial village, nuclear power and the jet engine have created the 20th century industrial village.

Stranton 🥬

As one drives past Stranton All Saints' church on the busy dual-carriageway on the way into Hartlepool, and smells the aroma of the beer brewing at the neighbouring Cameron's Brewery, it is difficult to envisage this ancient church as the centre of a tiny village.

The name Stranton derives from Strand-ton, the village by

the sea. Before West Hartlepool was built up Stranton was in fact by the sea. The parish church of All Saints was given by Robert de Brus to Guisborough Priory in 1129. The parish at that time also included Seaton Carew. In 1189 the lands were sold to the Bishop of Durham. The present church has no surviving Saxon features, although some parts date from the 12th century. Village life continued in the normal rural way, villagers rarely ventured farther than the nearby hamlets. The road from Stockton to Hartlepool passed through Stranton.

The population of Stranton was 371 in 1821, and it escalated rapidly in the next few years with the advent of the railways in 1832. The tiny hamlet of Newburn Raw adjoining Stranton was developed to accommodate the navvies who built the railway and the docks. Known at first as New Stranton it later became West Hartlepool, and it grew and grew. By 1851 the population of Stranton and New Stranton was over 4,000. This burgeoning town of West Hartlepool gradually engulfed the old Stranton village. Later census returns show that there were only a few born-Strantonians, the population hailed from every corner of the British Isles, Scandinavia and Germany.

Stranton parish council found it increasingly difficult to cope with this large and varied community. In 1854 the Board of Improvement was formed. At this time many people were living in wooden shanties. The Stranton churchyard, despite having been extended, was almost full. A new cemetery was opened, a new parish was formed and Christ church was built with the limestone excavated from the new docks. Another church, St James', was built in 1870.

Sadly today little of old Stranton survives. All Saints' church has recently been restored. The windmill clearly seen on old photographs has long since been replaced by brewery buildings. Next to the church stands the old Blacksmith's

Arms, it still has the tiny window overlooking the church-yard where watch was kept to prevent the bodysnatchers doing their dastardly deeds. Opposite the church stands Greenbank, built in the 19th century it was the home of J. W. Cameron. This mansion now houses the brewery offices. In front of this building the council have attempted to recreate the village green. Unfortunately it seems to be a haven for run-away trolleys.

To add confusion to where Stranton was, the outsider needs to appreciate that the village was completely engulfed by West Hartlepool, which ceased to exist in 1967, but present day residents believe the heart of Hartlepool is Stranton.

Thornaby 🦌

Thornaby village lies in an idyll of peace and quiet, the medieval village slumbering under a blanket of turf, sur-mounted by the Norman church and surrounded by Victo-rian and 20th century houses, the whole bypassed by the rush of traffic on Thornaby Road. The industrialisation in the 19th century took place to the east of the old village. The 20th century New Town was built to the south on, and adjacent to, the wartime aerodrome.

Thornaby green with its Norman church of St Peter must look much as it did 900 years ago. The church itself stands alone among the visible undulations of the buried medieval village. Inside the church the stonemason has left his trade-mark, a delicately carved mouse on the stonework which surrounds a window.

Thornaby did not change until the completion of the bridge over the Tees in 1771. This united south of the river,

152

which was in the North Riding, and Stockton which was in County Durham, and created the village of South Stockton, latterly called Thornaby. This area was the site of the 19th century industrialisation. The first census of 1801 shows the population of Thornaby was 167.

Stafford Pottery was established in 1825. A glass bottle factory was followed in 1840 by the Teesdale Iron Works. By 1851 the population was 1,759. The industrialisation of South Stockton continued at a rapid rate. In 1880 there were 18 public houses, but Thornaby village still had only 26 houses. The river bank and all the roads leading to it had many and various manufacturing establishments. There was the Yorkshire Iron Works, Mr Thwaites who made gloves and clothes from sheepskins, ropeworks, sawmills, herring curing, a taxidermist, and Mr Hill the butcher who was the first to import and sell Amercian beef. The previously mentioned glass bottle factory had its own jetty and sailing vessel which regularly sailed to the larger markets in London. South of this industrial area hundreds of terrace houses were built to house the growing workforce. In 1901 the population was more than 16,000.

Preceding the Second World War the Air Ministry bought 697 acres of land south of Thornaby village for development as an aerodrome. In 1962 the local authority bought 374 acres of this site to be developed as Thornaby New Town. A further 350 acres was entrusted to English Industrial Estates for the development of light industry to provide work for 10,000 people. The Victorian industries no longer exist. Thornaby village by this time was an oasis in an ever busier world.

Across Thornaby Road, opposite to the entrance to Thornaby village stands Thornaby Snooker Club. This was the officers' mess for the pilots flying out of Thornaby Aerodrome during the war. The upper two floors of the mess were the infirmary. It is reputed the site is haunted by the ghost of a Canadian pilot who was fatally injured trying to land his badly damaged plane.

Thornaby today is a mixture of old and new, and many people work out of the area, some on the North Sea oil rigs. There are still many rows of terrace houses near the old industrial area. The new housing estates on the old airfield are a mixture of local authority housing and private homes including semis, bungalows and substantial three and four bedroom detached dwellings. Thornaby village just north of this new conurbation is like a time capsule, quiet and peaceful, guarded by the Norman church of St Peter ad Vincula.

Thorpe Thewles ॐ

Built in 1877 to carry the Clarence Railway to Wynyard, Thorpe Thewles viaduct, a magnificent piece of Victorian architecture, once heralded the approach via the A177 to the village of Thorpe Thewles, located three miles north of Stockton and some 16 miles south of the city of Durham. Sadly this 460 yard long viaduct comprising 21 arches, having taken two and a half years hard labour to build, was demolished in two and a half seconds on 3rd June 1979, stripping the village of these regal and impressive arches and destroying with it some of our local railway heritage.

The village of Thorpe Thewles is the main centre of the agricultural parish of Grindon, an area of some 5,400 acres embracing the 2,500 acres of Wynyard Hall, the former seat of the Londonderry family. It is fortunate in that, unlike some other villages, much of the relatively recent development sits comfortably with the older part of the village and retains the settlement's character, which is an interesting variety of 17th, 18th and 19th century buildings.

The village, formerly Thorp Thewles, now spelt Thorpe Thewles, derived its name from a resident family. Matilda, daughter of Godefrid de Thorp, in about the year 1200 granted part of her lands to Stephen de Elwick, who by charter granted and gave all his lands in Thorp to the prior and monks of Finchale for the support of hospitality. Afterwards the Hiltons, Bulmers and Blakistons appear as proprietors in Thorp.

Despite the loss of the unmistakable landmark of the viaduct the village still retains features of historical and architectural merit. It possesses a church, two public houses, both of which are Grade II listed buildings, a manor house, a small shop, a village hall and a village green.

In every parish, the church building tells several stories. Such is the case of Thorpe Thewles – the original church of the parish was at Grindon and dedicated to St Thomas a Becket. Clearly the clash between King Henry and his archbishop is important not just for historians today, it mattered to the people of Grindon 800 years ago. Six centuries after Thomas' martyrdom, William Cassidi, the then vicar of Thorpe, saw the need for a new building on a new site and because of the movement of the population over the years from Grindon to the sand-quarrying at nearby Thorpe Thewles, a new church, the church of Holy Trinity, was built in 1848.

The former church at Grindon rapidly deteriorated and is now only a ruin, which, however, remains a Grade A listed building – a category into which only the top 4% of historical monuments fall. It is interesting to note the altar top and the stone font were removed from Grindon to the new church at Thorpe, leaving behind the flagstone on which it is alleged Thomas a Becket was murdered in Canterbury

Cathedral. However, the church of Holy Trinity encountered innumerable problems, so much so that a new church, this time the church of St James, was built on the foundations of the former Trinity church. Therefore, the present church of St James is relatively young and in 1987 a spectacular floral festival in the church heralded the celebratory centennial anniversary, with every aspect of life in the village being represented in floral presentations.

As a consequence of the close proximity of the stately home of Wynyard, also in Grindon parish, the village has enjoyed over the years the frequent visit of royals, semi-royals and leading statesmen and politicians from all over the world.

King Edward VII was a frequent visitor to Wynyard and held a privy council in the mirror room of Wynyard in 1902 – a commemorative plaque is still to be seen in that room. Royal shooting parties were often held at Wynyard. Ribbentrop's name is seen in the visitors book. Wellington was a frequent visitor and to commemorate his visit of 1827 an obelisk some 127 ft in height was erected in the Park.

The Duke of York, later King George VI paid a visit to Wynyard on the occasion of the opening of the Newport Bridge in 1934, alas in 1990 sadly bolted firmly never to rise above the river Tees again. Our present Queen, the then Princess Elizabeth made an overnight stay at Wynyard in the late 1940s having made an official engagement at Stockton. In September 1990 Mr and Mrs John Hall, the present owners of Wynyard Hall, entertained the former Prime Minister Mrs Margaret Thatcher.

Two other historic houses are situated on the outskirts of the village. Howden Hall is situated about three quarters of a mile from the village, built in 1735 as an 'off-shoot' of Wynyard for the fourth son of the fourth Marquis of Londonderry. Bought in 1904 by James Jenkins, who had strong connections with Nimmo's Brewery at Castle Eden and was involved in Hartlepool shipping, it is now farmed by the Duell family.

The site of Blakiston Hall still remains in Blakiston Lane, the once main road from Durham to Stockton. As at Wynyard Hall a ghost is alleged to haunt the property, and seems to have been sighted on occasions. A modern bungalow now stands on the Blakiston Hall site.

Being situated just outside the Borough of Stockton and adjacent to the very busy A177, the village presents itself as a very attractive location for commuters travelling to Teesside and the rapidly expanding north-east corner of England. As a consequence, there is considerable pressure for an expansion of the village and should this come, it is essential the character of the village is protected. Any development should take into consideration the whole of the central area of Thorpe Thewles, which is of great archaeological interest and should be preserved for future generations.

Upleatham 🦋

Upleatham, the village on the hill, or from the Norse definition, 'settlement on the upper slopes'. The village name has changed over the centuries, Uplider, Upeleder, Uplium, Uplithium to the present day spelling Upleatham. The highest point of the parish of Upleatham is Beacon Hill and it was here that Bronze Age men buried their chief. His body had been cremated and then put into a burial urn, accompanied by a smaller urn containing some decorative artefacts. The urns were buried in a shallow grave and there they lay undisturbed for 3,000 years.

A fragment of an Anglican cross found in the Old Church of Upleatham bears evidence that the village was Christian long before the Conquest. Robert de Brus gave the church at Upleatham to the Priory at Guisborough. The villagers paid their tithes to the priory, in return they were assured of the services of a canon/priest to carry out all the church duties such as baptisms, marriages and burials.

Over the centuries the village has moved up the hill, originating at the foot of the hill, possibly in and around the site of the Old Church. The first village had a church and 24 dwellings. This was the church and village that the Danes destroyed, and Christianity fell into abeyance until another Dane, Earl Siward owned Upleatham and gradually the Christian church returned.

The Old Church of Upleatham stands beside the road that stretches from Guisborough to Saltburn. It is supposed to be the smallest church in England but this is a misnomer. The present building is only 18 ft long by 15 ft wide, but this is only the remains of a once larger church. This little church was built in 1684, and includes a small tower and a part of the nave. After the main part of the church was demolished in 1822, the remaining part of the building was used as a mortuary chapel for burials in the Old Churchyard. Inside this diminutive building there are some diamond shaped tablets displaying the coats of arms of the Dundas family. In 1966 this small church was falling into even greater state of disrepair. An article written by the noted local historian, Alex Wright decrying this neglect led to a company of soldiers from the Green Howards volunteering to do restoration work on the church. When the work was completed there was a service of rededication. A plaque was unveiled by Mrs Wharton of Skelton Castle thanking the Green Howards.

The Earl of Zetland gave the laundry from Upleatham Hall for use as the first school. He paid an allowance of £12 a year to the headmaster, and £10 a year to the headmistress.

They also received two pence or three pence a week paid by the pupils. In 1822 there were 22 boys and girls, and by 1863 this number had risen to 40.

Because of the steepness of the land, the farmers used oxen to pull the ploughs until the beginning of the 20th century. These animals were more placid than the usual shire horses and whereas a horse faced with the land dropping away at an acute angle would become quite skittish the oxen remained calm. Sir Thomas Dundas experimented with stock improvement by cross breeding.

The rural calm of Upleatham was rudely shattered with the discovery of a rich seam of iron ore. This was 13 ft thick, and it was estimated that it would produce over 36 million tons of ore. The mines opened in 1851 and eventually employed 500 men and boys. The Upleatham mine was reputed to be the best in the world, producing high grade ore in seams eight to 13 ft thick. The village prospered and the population increased threefold. By the beginning of the 20th century the ravages of the mining were blatantly obvious. Many cottages, a place of worship and Upleatham Hall had all fallen victim of land subsidence. The mine closed in three stages, 1912, 1921, and 1923. The land where the Hall stood has been landscaped and planted with trees, though the yew trees that grew on and around the lawn of the Hall are still there.

The walled garden is now a commercial enterprise. The village still suffers from subsidence of the land. In 1936 the Reverend Thomas Walters wrote a booklet entitled *Sweet Upleatham*. This so aptly describes the setting and appeal of Upleatham village.

Whitton 🌿

In 1801 Whitton was classified as a hamlet, with five farms and one public house, which no longer exists. At one time there were only 38 inhabitants. The owners of the hamlet were the Vane-Tempest branch of the Londonderry family. More houses were built when the Dorman-Long Company opened the Carlton Ironworks at the neighbouring village now known as Stillington. The influx of families to work at the ironworks were mainly housed at Whitton, in a row of cottages known as Millbank Terrace. The men had to walk three quarters of a mile over fields to get to work; shopping had to be done at Stillington as well, there were no shops at Whitton. To travel elsewhere the only means of transport was to walk, cycle, if you had one, or use a pony and trap to carry you to the nearest station and get the train to your desired destination.

At one end of Whitton village was a pond where the local farmers watered their horses and cattle. When frozen in winter this pond was an ideal place to skate. In the centre of the village was a gravel pit. This had white fencing around it for many years, but recently the fencing was removed and the infilled pit allowed to become grass covered.

A bungalow in the village known as 'Old Shakespeares' (no connection with the great William) belonged to a Mr Shakespear, who kept a beautiful garden. Further down the road was a detached house owned by a railway worker who also had a beautiful garden. Just beyond this house was a steep bank leading over a bridged stream which is the dividing line between Whitton and Bishopton. There are several scattered houses and three farms here, the end farm is adjacent to the road which to the north leads to Carlton Ironworks, and to the south leads to Redmarshall.

To the south of the village is a steep bank known as

Cobblers Bank near to which was the pump which was the main supply of drinking water for the villagers. Three cottages stood at the top of Cobblers Bank and behind them was the fourth farm and Whitton House, reputedly the home of nobility. A small plantation nearby was an exciting and safe place where children could play, and the fifth farm was located close by.

Whitton is a happy and contented place in which to live and has not changed much in the last 70 years. Electricity was not installed until the 1930s. Prior to that candles and oil lamps were the only form of lighting. Coal fired ranges incorporating ovens were the only form of heating and cooking. Those ranges with an integral boiler also heated water. Coal was delivered by horse and cart. Many other necessities were delivered in this way, including the Sunday joint. Thank heaven for modern science which has modernised our way of life and retained our rural setting.

Wilton ஒ

Driving towards Redcar from Eston along the A174 one can't miss the sprawling complex of ICI chemical industry on the left hand side of the road. The observant driver might also notice the sign which says Wilton Village and another which says Wilton Castle. Those who make the detour find a delightful village whose picturesque appearance reveals little of its vibrant history. In fact it remains much as its owner Sir John H. Lowther described it in 1830.

'Here Wilton stands, the subject of my lays;
In woods embossed shines her fair domain
Where calm content and peaceful pleasures reign
Where chastened art and lavish nature vie
With blended charms to fascinate the eye . . .'

Needless to say this gem of a village stands on the right hand side of the A174, cradled at the foot of the Eston Hills.

Wilton church, typically Norman in design, has two effigies in the porch, a knight and a lady, possibly members of the Bulmer family. The Bulmers settled at Wilton shortly after the Norman Conquest. They built a manor house, which Sir Ralph de Bulmer, circa 1330, with the consent of Edward III, fortified and strengthened. Cleveland was constantly threatened by the marauding Scots in the 13th and 14th centuries. In fact the Bulmers were fighting the Scots until the 16th century. Sir William Bulmer, under the command of the Earl of Surrey, met and defeated the Scots at Flodden Field in 1513.

Sir John Bulmer was prominent in the protest against Henry VIII's religious reformation and the consequential closing of the monasteries. The rising of 1536, known as 'The Pilgrimage of Grace', captured York, Pontefract and Hull under the leadership of the Bulmers, Percys and the Archbishop of York. A shortlived and peaceful solution was arranged, then further violence erupted. The King quickly and ruthlessly quashed this rebellion. Sir John Bulmer was hanged at Tyburn and Lady Bulmer was burned at the stake at Smithfield. All the Bulmers' possessions were confiscated by the Crown. A ghost of a lady, accompanied by a spaniel, has been seen on the stairs of Wilton Castle, which stands on the site of the original manor house. Is this the ghost of the ill-fated Lady Bulmer? Religious discontent continued in Cleveland until 1567 when a Catholic rebellion was aborted.

Upon the accession of Elizabeth I, many Northern townships including Wilton were granted Royal Pardons. At the same time, the Queen's men rode north in the depths of winter, sentenced and hanged all those not included in the pardon. The Queen granted the Wilton estate to Lord Cornwallis. Later it was inherited by Lord Holland and passed to the Lowther family. The Lowthers owned it until it was bought by ICI in the latter days of the Second World War. Neglected for centuries the original castle (fortified manor house) was in ruins. A 17th century eye witness said 'it was so ruinous to present little to the eye of the traveller but its mouldering tower'. The new Wilton Castle is a fine example of romantic Gothic architecture, built about 1806–1807.

The discovery of iron ore in the hills south of the castle was the first industrial intrusion near to Wilton village. Because of the ore taken out by the miners the area is 'honeycombed' and subject to subsidence. Consequently it is not suitable for development. ICI have, since they purchased the land, tamed the wild moorland hill tops behind the castle. At first they put several species of pigs out on the land to root out the unwanted bracken, brambles and other weeds. This made the land suitable for sowing as pasture land, which today supports crossbred Charolais and shorthorn cattle. In difficult places timber is grown.

The castle, the headquarters of ICI's social amenities, has an 18 hole golf course. To the west of the site the local authorities have developed a nature trail. Wilton village, hidden by its shroud of trees, lies quietly untouched by the 20th century.

Wolviston

Many people knew Wolviston well in the early 1970s, not so much for its beauty as a village but as a bottleneck on the main A19 trunk road which passed through the village. This road originated as a turnpike from Stockton to Sunderland and formed the High Street, eventually becoming the main road from Selby to Sunderland.

In older times the High Street supported six inns supplying

travellers with their needs and stabling facilities. The growth of transport and population in the Teesside area in the 1950s and 1960s led to the construction of the first bypass on the east side of the village. Further gains were made when the second bypass for Billingham and Wolviston was constructed in the 1970s. This gives an island character to the village, separated from urban Billingham by green belt and bypasses.

Wolviston has been in existence since Saxon times under a variety of names, including Wolfstun and Ulvestun before the current spelling was adopted. It was essentially a farming community close to the estates of Lord Londonderry, other employment being available at local salt wells and brick works. Besides the six farms and six inns, there were general dealers, ironmongers, blacksmiths, butchers (and slaughterhouse) and a fish and chip shop. The oldest farmhouse was Sundial Farm, 1723, now modernised as a domestic dwelling.

The arrival of the chemical industry in nearby Billingham in the 1920s changed that village from a rural community to a company town, and further expansion after the Second World War saw Billingham expand rapidly, becoming an urban area. The comparative calm of Wolviston meant that it was an attractive place to live, and those areas of the village available were built on. Over the years the shops in the village have had to close and villagers are now left with three farms, two pubs, a post office and general dealer, an off licence, a fashion shop and very few buses. The population is now around 800 and not likely to increase significantly as the only building space available now is to infill small sites within the village. Wolviston Hall, used as a prisoner of war camp in the Second World War, was demolished to make way for 30 houses.

The nature of the village has changed from a rural one to

middle class residential with people from the legal and medical professions and local businesses. This has tended to strengthen the village community and generates a good community spirit within the village, with a WI, over sixties club, gardening society, a ladies section and village association. Sports are catered for by the cricket club, riding school and tennis club. The village hall is used for various activities. The spirit is best exampled by the success of the village in nationwide Tidy Village and Britain in Bloom competitions.

The village today comprises 19th century terraced housing with modern detached developments. Almshouses were instituted by the Marchioness of Londonderry in 1838. They are now used by pensioners of the village. Extra modern bungalows were built for pensioners around the small park opposite the post office. There are spacious greens and the requisite well-stocked duck pond which unfortunately in these modern times has been depleted around Christmas time. The traditional village Feast Day, held on the first Sunday after Lammas Day in July, was started in the 19th century and survives today in a different form. The day after would be given to a horticultural show, races and games for the children with a dance at the local pubs on the evening for the parents. The modern version still has the accent on the children's games with displays and fund raising stalls.

There has been a church in the village since the 12th century, the present one dating from 1876. Two chapels were constructed in the 19th century, the older Wesleyan chapel in 1829 now serves as the meeting place for the gardening society.

Schools were introduced in 1811 and 1836, with the present one built in 1877 with school house facing the larger of the two village greens. Approximately 100 pupils attend, these being drawn from the parish rather than the village.

The village school has a good friendly atmosphere and is well supported by parents within the community.

The other green, Black Railing Green, is triangular and is named after the low black iron fence surrounding it. The village war memorial is located at its apex.

Yarm 🦢

Yarm is the birthplace of the railways. On the wall of the George and Dragon inn is a plaque, stating the date and the names of the originators of the first railway in the world, the Darlington to Stockton. Even today Yarm is embraced by the railway viaduct, consisting of 43 arches. Over seven million bricks were used in its construction. Many more bricks were added when it was reinforced between the wars. Walk through one of the Wynds to appreciate the magnificence of this structure, created by Thomas Grainger in 1849.

Yarm is a peninsula with water, the river Tees, on three sides. The river is still the boundary for the parish, deanery and diocese. Prior to the 1974 boundary changes Yarm was in Yorkshire, a finger of land jutting into Durham. Today it is in Cleveland.

The river has always been important and before Stockton and later Middlesbrough, Yarm was the main landing place on the Tees for cargo ships. Because of its location and with no point more than 25 ft above sea level, Yarm has been subject to frequent flooding. The level of various floods is marked on the town hall and other buildings in Yarm. Pleasure steamers made the journey from Middlesbrough to Yarm on a Sunday afternoon as late as the 1920s. Also on the banks of the river is the skinyard. In the 19th century this company washed the skins in the river, the men working from floats. Later these floats were used when the river was the only place where you could learn to swim. With the increase in house building during the 1930s this pastime and boating ceased because of increased pollution of the water. In recent times the river has been greatly improved, some boating takes place, but the main sport is angling, organised by the Yarm Angling Club. The skinyard is now closed and imaginative landscaping is planned for the banks of the Tees.

Yarm Town Hall

Travelling north the wide high street ends at the bridge built by Bishop Skilaw of Durham circa 1400. It is the oldest bridge still in daily use. The riverside path passes underneath. The first span is called the Sandspan because of the large amount of sand deposited there by the ebb and flow of the tide. The footpath along the river around Yarm is called True Lovers Walk.

Number 17 The High Street was the home of the Merry-wethers, who entertained John Wesley when he came to open the Methodist chapel in 1768. A rare octagonal building, John Wesley described it as one of the finest buildings in England. Bridge House has an underground passage, and also in the High Street is Tom Brown's house. He was the hero of Dettingham. Recently a fine tombstone has been erected in the churchyard to mark this hero's resting place. There is some controversy whether this house or Hope House is the oldest in Yarm.

The parish church of St Mary Magdalene was rebuilt in 1730. The tower and the west end are the oldest parts, but the vestry was only built in 1906. The Moses window was designed by William Pecket of York in 1768. This window, the 15th century font and the oak pews add to the beauty of the church.

At the south end of the High Street stands the Catholic church, which was built by the Meynell family who lived in the nearby house called the Friarage. This is the site of the monastery used by the Black Friars. An old Tudor dovecote stands in the grounds. The Friarage is now part of Yarm school. The first school in Yarm, 400 years ago, was in St Mary's churchyard. It then moved to Grammar School Lane in 1884.

King John granted a charter for Yarm to hold a fair in October every year. The chairman of the council reads the fair charter on the third Saturday in October. This charter is for the sale of cattle, horses, sheep and cheese. The fair is still held, but now it is mostly amusements, roundabouts and fortune tellers, with token horse trading, all laid out in the High Street.

Last of all there is a castle in Yarm, majestic in detail. If you look closely you will find it in West Street, on the wall of Commondale House opposite the church. A building that is not missed is the town hall. It stands in the centre of the High Street. Originally built on open arches as a market cross it is now enclosed and is topped by a fine clock and weathervane. The council chamber is little changed.

The High Street is mainly Georgian, with a good mix of food shops, antiques emporiums, male and female boutiques and other unique businesses, as well as the usual financial houses. Mainly a dormitory for the business areas of Cleveland, Yarm is an interesting place to live.

Yearby 🍂

In Mr Ord's fact finding tour of 1846, Yearby in the parish of Kirkleatham is described as 'a small hamlet scarcely deserving any separate notice'. Further investigation however shows this tiny hamlet to have had an interesting and sometimes controversial history.

In the early to mid 1700s Sir Charles Turner of Kirkleatham Hall did much to improve living and agricultural conditions in the surrounding area. Finding most of the cottages in Yearby to be 'wretched hovels, placed every where except in convenient positions' he built new cottages in brick and tile and placed them round an open space in the most attractive manner, including shops and dwellings for the tradespeople. Records tell us that the district at that time

169

was 'much pestered with a collection of little blackguard ale houses which encouraged idleness and drunkenness among the villagers and were the haunts of the smugglers who frequented the coast'. Charles Turner demolished these and built two new inns, one being situated close to Yearby.

There was a school in Yearby before 1840 which was supported by the local manor for the sum of £291 5 shillings per year, where 35 to 40 children were taught reading, writing and arithmetic. Records in 1861 give details of three boarders – the youngest a mere three years of age.

During restoration work in 1976 to convert the schoolhouse into a private dwelling, a ten ft well was discovered under the floor boards. Research found the well had quite a history. At the end of the 19th century when an epidemic of enteric fever swept Teesside, due to the population drinking polluted water from the river Tees, the villagers of Yearby were kept free from sickness because they had their own supply of fresh water direct from this and other wells in the village.

A strange and unexplained fact came to light in the census of 1841: although there were only 36 houses (three unoccupied) and 153 inhabitants, there were no less than twelve shoemakers! It is amusing to note that on census day one Charles Emmerson was not at home (it was Stokesley races and quite a number of Clevelanders were away when the enumerator called).

Yearby hit the headlines in 1954 when fragments of two pottery vessels (representing the coarse tableware of the late 17th century) were uncovered during ploughing at Yearby Farm. These were found to contain 1,197 assorted silver coins dating from 1551–1697. An inquest held in Redcar the following week declared the find to be treasure trove and the coins are now in the British Museum.

An interesting but unproved theory as to why the coins

170

were there centres around a pigeon cote (now preserved as a building of architectural and historic interest). The cote was used to breed pigeons for shooting, a very popular sport of bygone days. At such sport the landed gentry from miles around gathered and heavy drinking and gambling took place. The pot could have been a 'kitty' – stolen by a thief who hid it under the hedge and perhaps did not dare return for it or couldn't find it.

The cote would have housed hundreds of pigeons; and as well as pigeon being a delicacy for the table, people were known to have travelled from miles around to obtain the dung, which was good for the land and was also used in the tanning of upper leather for shoes, and indeed formerly saltpetre was collected from it.

Controversy came to thousand year old Yearby in 1973 when the then Teesside Council decided to make Yearby a smoke free zone. Objectors attempted to uphold the ancient right (dating to the times when Yearby was surrounded by forest) of villagers to burn log fires on their inglenook fireplaces, but although over 6,000 deeds regarding Yearby and its peculiar rural area perks were found in archives at Northallerton, they did eventually lose their appeal.

More publicity for Yearby came in 1982 when a local hermit was evicted from a 'mine shaft' in Yearby woods. In fact though the structure did resemble the entrance to a drift mine it was in fact an old ice house (probably built to serve the Turners of Kirkleatham Hall) and by the mid 1850s had already acquired some age. Such buildings were designed to hold large quantities of ice and snow and could store meat for several months. It was probably situated at that spot as it was quite close to the Yearby fish ponds. It is thought that the building could have been used at a later date as an explosives magazine for the nearby Dunsdale ironstone mine but this is not confirmed.

Modern day Yearby, once mainly agricultural, now has only one active farm and has become increasingly residential. It consists of two rows of houses with long front gardens, extending to the road, which has a pavement of diamond patterned scoria blocks. Although adjacent to a busy main road and in very close proximity to the giant ICI chemical complex, Yearby retains a tranquil old world charm. It became a conservation area in 1974.

Old Cottages, Eston

Index